The Recipes of Musa Dagh

AN ARMENIAN COOKBOOK
IN A DIALECT OF ITS OWN

The Recipes of
VICTORIA CHAPARIAN MAGZANIAN

by Alberta, Anna and Louisa Magzanian

The Recipes of Musa Dagh

Copyright © 2008 Alberta, Anna and Louisa Magzanian
All rights reserved

http://www.lulu.com/content/4356800

Published by: Lulu Press

No portion of this book may be reproduced — mechanically, electronically, or by any other means, including photocopying — without written permission of the authors.

Cover and interior design, food photography and map by Richard Furno except others as credited.

ISBN 9 780557 016136

Cover photos

Mom's Recipes

As she prepared them in
Bitias, Syria (now Turkey)

As well as in
Syria,
Lebanon,
New Jersey

And finally in
Olney, Maryland

Victoria Magzanian

Dedication

To Mom (1906-1988)
Victoria Chaparian Magzanian
for cooking heritage

and Pop (1888-1986)
Samuel HaGop Magzanian
for growing food and stone walls

The Recipes of Musa Dagh

Contents

Preserving Distinctive Armenian Recipes — 9

Beverages — 18
    Demitasse Coffee — 19
    Yogurt Drink — 19

Yogurts & Cheeses — 21
    Yogurt — 22
    Yogurt Cheese or Drained Yogurt — 23
    String Cheese — 23
    Ann's Cottage Cheese — 25
    Ann's Cottage Cheese Spread — 25
    Dried Cheese Balls — 26

Breads — 27
    Breakfast Rolls — 28
    Cheese Bread — 29
    Flaky Coil Bread — 30
    Holiday Rings — 32
    Cheese Boerek — 34
    Unleavened Flat Bread — 35

Appetizers — 37
    Hummus — 38
    Baba Ghanoush — 38

Salads — 40
    Potato Salad — 41
    Fava Beans with Yogurt — 41
    Red Kidney Bean Salad — 42
    Red Bean Salad — 42
    Tabouli — 42
    Bulgur Salad with Cooked Vegetables — 43
    Garden Salad — 44
    Yogurt with Eggplant — 44
    Watercress Salad — 45
    Eggplant and Walnut Salad — 45

Soups & Stews — 47
    Cooked Skinless Whole Wheat — 48
    Cabbage Soup or Soup de Paris — 48
    Split Red Lentil Soup — 49
    Lentil Soup Variation with Cayenne — 50
    Galagacia Soup — 50
    White Bean Soup — 51

Potato Multi-Bean Soup	52
Swiss Chard with Multi-Bean Soup	53
Tomato Soup	54
Vegetable Soup	54
Head and Tongue Soup	55
Tongue and Tripe Soup	56
Soups with Dumplings	**57**
Yogurt Soup	58
Dumplings: for Yogurt Soup	58
Dumplings for Soups	60
Yogurt Soup with Bulgur-meat Dumplings	61
Tomato Soup with Dumplings	62
Cold Soups	**63**
Yogurt Soup with Skinless Whole Wheat	63
Yogurt Lentil Pilaf Soup	63
Cucumber Soup	64
Stews	**64**
Green Bean, Potato and Zucchini Stew	64
Yogurt, Zucchini and Meat Stew	65
Okra Stew	66
Multi-Legume Stew	66
Chick Peas with Eggplant	67
Eggplant with Meat	68
Meat with Green Beans	69

Vegetables   70

Potatoes	**71**
Potatoes with Sautéed Onions	71
Potato with Bulgur	71
Potato with Skinless Whole Wheat	72
Other Vegetables	**73**
Spinach with Onions	73
Mixed Beans with Walnuts	73
Fava Beans with Onions	74
Onion Salad	74
Grilled Tomatoes	75
Grilled Vegetables	75
Grilled Corn on the Cob	75
Roasted Eggplant	76
Parsley and Egg Patties	76
Baked Eggplant with Tomato and Garlic	77
Fried Eggplant	77
Fried Eggplant with Eggs	78
Fried Zucchini	78

Pilaf   80

Rice Pilaf	81
Bulgur Pilaf with Chick Peas	81
Pilaf with Meat	82

Fava Bean Pilaf 83
Potato Bulgur Pilaf 83
Green Bean Bulgur Pilaf 84
Bean-Potato Bulgur Pilaf 85
Mixed Vegetable Pilaf 85
Lentil Pilaf 86

Stuffed Vegetables — 87

Fillings (Kima) — **88**
Meat filling 88
Meatless Rice Filling 89
Meatless Bulgur Filling 89

The Stuffed Vegetables — **90**
Stuffed Grape Leaves 90
Stuffed Cabbage Leaves 91
Stuffed Eggplant, Zucchini & Yellow Squash 91
Stuffed Peppers 92
Stuffed Tomatoes 93
Stuffed Swiss Chard 94

Meat Dishes — 95

Baked Vegetables with Meat 96
Baked Dumplings 96
Shish Kebab 98
Ground Meat Kebab 99
Kebab with Eggplant 100
Liver Kebab 100
Barbecued Chicken 100
Meat Pizza 101
Musa Dagh Martadella 103
Lamb with Skinless Whole Wheat 104
Barbecued Lamb Chops 104
Eggplant Boats 105
Tripe 106
Stewed Liver 107
Stuffed Shoulder of Lamb 108
Bachelor's Feast or Father's Specialty 109

Keufteh — **109**
Musa Dagh Steak Tartare 109
Keufteh Common Ingredients 110
Diamond-shaped Pie 111
Stuffed Torpedo-shaped Meatballs 113

Top-Tope: 3 Keufteh variations — **114**
Stuffed Bulgur-Meat Patties 114
Stuffed Parsley-Walnut Patties 115
Plain Bulgur Patties 115

Token Fish — 116

Fish du Jour 117

Pickles, Relish & Sauces — 118

- Green Olives — 119
- Ripe Black Olives — 120
- Drained Yogurt with Sautéed Onions — 120
- Pepper Paste — 120
- Pink Pickles — 121
- Summer Pickles — 122
- Tomato Relish or Sauce — 122
- Yogurt-Garlic Sauce — 123
- Lemon Juice-Garlic Sauce — 123
- Canned Grape Leaves — 123

Snacks — 125

- Roasted Seeds — 126
- Roasted Chick Peas — 126
- Roasted Dry Chick Peas — 127
- Fresh Wheat Berries — 127

Desserts — 128

- Sugar Water Syrup — 129
- Rice Pudding — 129
- Young Walnut Preserve — 130
- Shredded Pastry with Walnuts — 131
- Shredded Pastry With Cheese — 133
- Boiled Wheat Berries — 133
- Molasses or Honey Dessert with Bulgur — 133
- Milk Yogurt Desert — 134
- Butter Cookies — 134
- Fruit Juice Pudding — 135
- Farina Pudding — 136
- Farina Pudding with Cheese — 136
- Fried Dumplings with Syrup — 136

Baklava — 139
- Baklava — 139
- Phyllo Rolls — 140
- Bird's Nest or Rosette Baklava — 141
- Coiled Baklava — 142

Epilogue — 144

Glossary — 165

Index — 167

Preserving Distinctive Armenian Recipes

by Alberta Magzanian

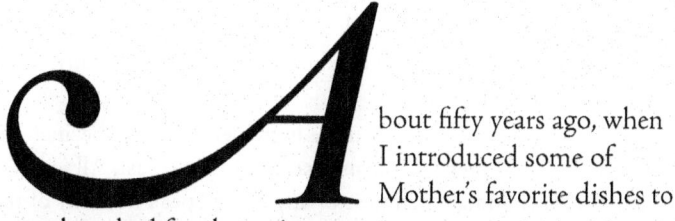

About fifty years ago, when I introduced some of Mother's favorite dishes to a college roommate, she asked for the recipes.

"Recipes? What recipes? We don't have recipes," I responded.

"What if I want to make some of these dishes? How do I go about it?" she asked.

"You just go to the kitchen and experiment," I answered lamely.

"Experiment? Do you realize how many generations have worked to perfect these dishes? If they don't get written down, they'll be lost," she admonished.

She was certainly correct, but I didn't have any interest at the time to start writing down recipes. Over several decades and with other friendly suggestions as well as random, hasty scribblings on various scraps, my sisters Anna and Louisa began to think that we should record the recipes of Mom's dishes. The final push came when Louisa's son kidded his Mom, "I think it's time to pass the baton. You and Anna need to teach me how to make these dishes."

It turns out he was serious. He has started to cook through the only medium we had – Anna's (somewhat impatient) tutoring!

Countless cookbooks line shelves in book stores, so why does the world need another one? Many tout the benefits of Mediterranean cooking similar to what has long been our diet. While many of our dishes are the same as other Middle Eastern and Armenian meals, many from Musa Dagh, the area we called home, are unique.

So we finally launched into our project! We divided the chores. Anna's role was clear. She had been Mom's diligent student, and had learned to cook while at her side and in exactly the same way—she used no measuring spoons or cups. My role was to deconstruct her methods and record each recipe as she cooked. I would interrupt Anna again and again so I could measure the handfuls and pinches of everything that went into each creation. All our lives, she had loved chiding me about how clueless I was of what preparation went into the dishes we ate. Now, she could do it through the entire process. "Wow!", she would say, "After all the years of eating this, NOW, you want to see how it is prepared?" This became a mantra in our kitchen.

With ingredients measured and preparation described, I fed the results to Louisa. She typed, organized, edited, wrote and rewrote. Then Anna and I would fill in the gaps she had found. Finally, her husband, Richard, turned our work into an attractive cookbook.

But Louisa insisted on one more ingredient. Though recipes are the subject of our book, food preparation also has links to the past. All foods of the world, whether French, Italian, Chinese or any other, speak not only of recipes, but of history, tradition, myths, people and geography. There are, in fact, few of us left to tell the Armenian stories of our "old country" of Musa Dagh—no Armenian now lives in our village of Bitias.

Anna and I grew up in Bitias during the 1920's and 30's, then left in 1939 along with nearly all the other Armenians of the region. Louisa is the youngest member of the family and the only one who wasn't born in our village. As she grew up she heard all the stories of people, relatives, traditions, events and much more of our village in the foothills of Musa Dagh. Having missed the opportunity to record the stories of our parents and relatives, Anna and I became her last hope to get them on paper. She also felt strongly that the recipes and the stories of where they came from are of a piece.

Telling the tales suits me well. I've spent my life reading, studying and teaching history. Here is a brief account of a small, coastal area and a tiny village called Bitias, from where these recipes came. More details are in the Epilogue.

The Recipes of Musa Dagh

Musa Dagh is a mountain located on the coast of the northeast corner of the Mediterranean Sea. It means "moun-

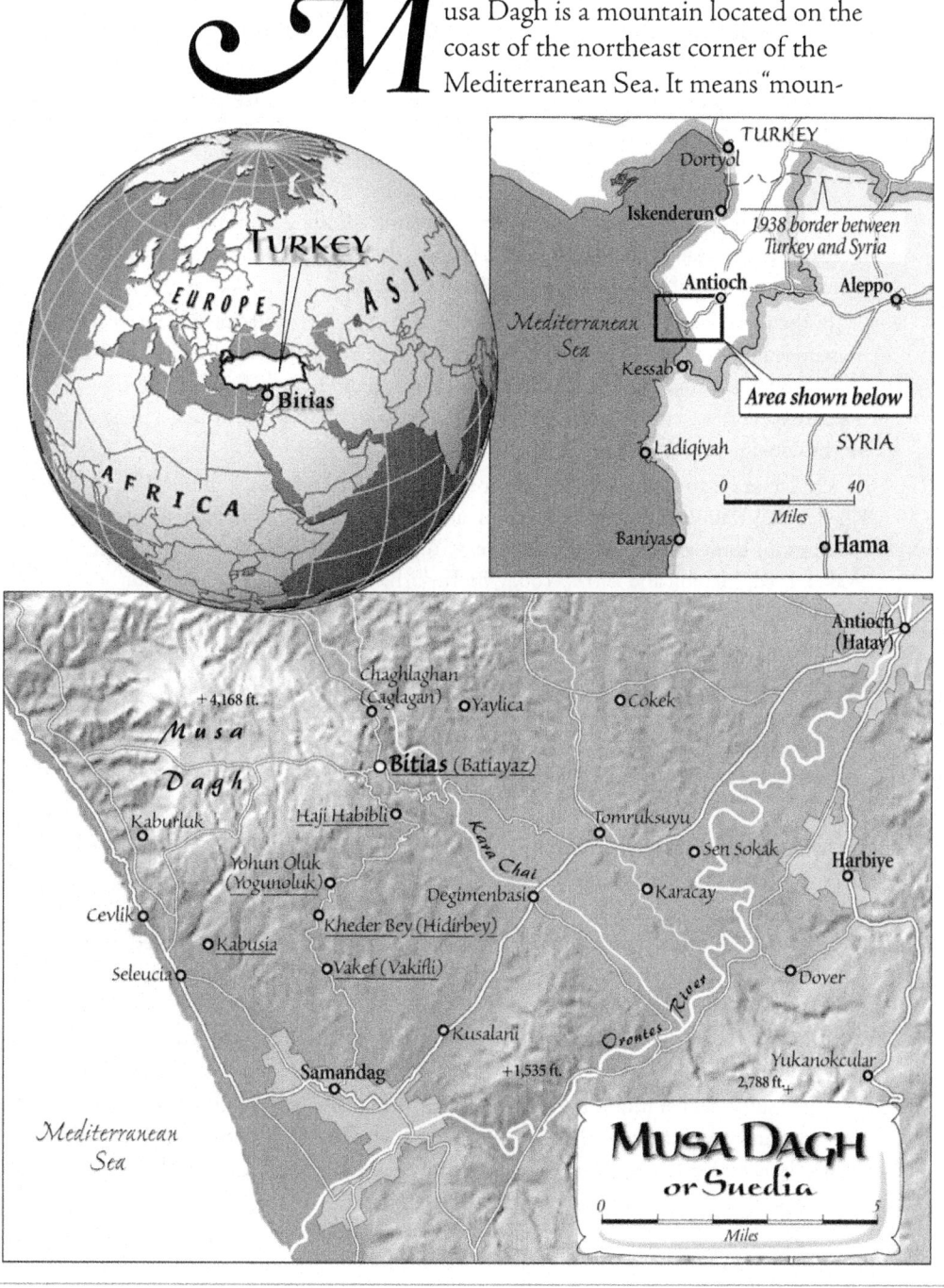

tain of Moses." But when asked, our parents and their contemporaries would say they came from "Suedia," the larger area around the mountain. "Suedia" stems from the name of one of Alexander the Great's generals, Seleucus. In his time, Seleucus founded several cities, among them Antioch on the Orontes River, as one of his capitals in Syria, and Seleucia on the Mediterranean coast.

Antioch, the closest true city near Bitias, became a leading administrative, commercial and cultural center of the region. During the early Christian era Antioch was the mission center of the followers of Jesus of Nazareth.

In the more than two millennia since Alexander, Antioch and Suedia saw rulers of many cultures—the Romans, Byzantines, Arabs, Crusaders from Europe, Seljuks and Ottomans from Asia, French after World War I and today's Turkish rule. The mixture of all these cultures certainly left their imprint on our region and, I imagine, on the cooking as well.

On Musa Dagh's flanks are the major villages of, in Armenian, Yohun Oluk, Kheder Bey, Kabusia, Vakef, Haji Habibli and our own village of Bitias. Many other spellings for these villages can be found; e.g., Yoghonoluk, Khodr Bey, Kaboussieh, Wakef, Hedj Habibli and Bitias. Today, in Turkish, you'll see Yogunoluk, Hidirbey, Kapisuyu, Vakifli, Haji Habibli and Batiayaz.

The mountain was known to us as "Musa Ler" in Armenian. It is "Jebel Musa" in Arabic. Today, its Turkish name is "Musa Dagi" or strictly "Musa Dağı". Because of its significance in history and in literature, our area is referred to as "Musa Dagh". Our language is quite distinct from standard Armenian. It's called "Kristinik," which, amusingly, means "Christian."

Musa Dagh gained its fame during World War I when the Armenians of our villages resisted an Ottoman deportation order. In 1914, the Great War, or World War I, erupted in Europe with the Ottoman Empire as an ally of the Central Powers of Germany and Austria. The following year, the Ottoman authorities embarked on a policy of forced deportation of the Armenians throughout Turkey. Horrible news of massacres were heard by the Armenian inhabitants of Suedia, and on July 28, 1915, the order for their own deportation arrived from Antioch. They were given seven days to comply.

After some deliberations, the leaders of the Musa Dagh villages decided to ignore the order and take refuge on their mountain to defend themselves. Some considered such a decision foolhardy, but the majority preferred an honorable death to desert marches across Syria with poor survival odds.

The villagers climbed Musa Dagh and took up defensive positions in its dense forests. They ferried what little food, arms and ammunition they could carry up the mountain. They dug trenches, set up scouts and waited for the inevitable attack of the Ottoman army. They had one advantage. They knew the mountain.

Amazingly, for more than fifty days, they successfully defended themselves against several Ottoman army attacks. At the same time, being adjacent to the sea, they made attempts to signal passing ships to alert them of their desperate situation and need for evacuation. The Ottomans had requested a more substantial force which would have clearly been able to overrun the Armenian positions. But before the reinforcements arrived, the French battleship *Guichen* responded to the rebel signals and, with six other ships, evacuated over 4,000 Armenians. They were taken to Port Said in Egypt where they stayed for the duration of the war.

The defense of their small homeland gained fame after World War I and was later popularized by Franz Werfel's 1934 novel *The Forty Days of Musa Dagh*. Though fictionalized, Werfel researched and followed the events in the villages and on the mountain fairly accurately. Because of his work, the Turkish name "Musa Dagh," became famous.

The original account of the Armenian defense of Musa Dagh and their evacuation was recorded and published by Rev. Dikran Antreassian, a leader of the revolt.

Our Father and two brothers had gone to America years before the war on the advice of their father who predicted another pogrom as had occurred in 1909. Most other relatives, on both sides of our extended family, went up the mountain. Mom, age 9, her two sisters and a younger brother were with them. Pop's grandmother started but didn't make it to the top.

However, older members of our families waited in the village in hopes that the order's enforcement could be halted. A small, male delegation from Bitias had gone to Antioch to plead their cause with their Turkish friends in high places. In the meantime, Ottoman soldiers began their occupation of Bitias. The Turkish authorities in Antioch, though friends of our family, could not interfere with the orders issued from Constantinople. At least they protected the delegation on their return home.

Upon their arrival, they and those who had waited for them were ready to join their compatriots. It was not to be. The mountain had been surrounded by the Ottoman army. They had no choice but to follow the deportation order. The few family members who were already on the mountain, including our mother, were smuggled

Some of the more than 4,000 Armenian refugees are seen here on deck of the "Guichen" in 1915. Many of our relatives were among them.

down along secret trails in the dead of night. The following day, 65 Evangelical families from Bitias joined their compatriots from other Musa Dagh villages on their way to Antioch.

Once in Antioch, government agents confiscated all the beasts of burden—horses, mules, donkeys—and forced the people to discard most of their meager possessions. Also in Antioch, a dear Turkish friend and business partner Hadji Mohammed (I don't remember his full name) met Mom's family, treated them to refreshments and volunteered to safe keep some of their valuables, all the while pleading with the soldiers but unable to change the course of events. He even marched with the family for two miles carrying some shoes and a bag of salt for their journey. Thus, the family marched on leaving behind their friend with tears streaming down his cheeks.

They marched for seven days until they reached Hama, an old and impoverished town in Syria. Within days of their arrival, Ottoman authorities rounded up all able-bodied men, Mom's two older brothers included, and shipped them to different parts of the empire as slave laborers. No one heard from them for the duration of the war and the family presumed them dead.

The women and children were left in Hama to fend for themselves. Mom, her mother, three older sisters, a younger brother and a sister-in-law with her infant son moved into a room with two other families each huddled in their own corner. Within months, weakened by starvation, many people began to succumb to diseases.

Four years later, Mom and her older sister were the only two family members of ten to survive in Hama. Months after the war's end, the two older brothers who had been forced into slave brigades rejoined their sisters.

Meanwhile, in 1915, Pop's immediate family also numbered ten. Pop and two brothers were in America and avoided the genocide but not the rest of his family. In 1919, of those seven in Bitias, only a brother and his nine year-old son were left alive.

In 1918, the Ottoman Empire defeated, the Middle East map was redrawn and Mom with her bothers and sister returned to Antioch before returning home to Bitias in 1920. While there, they were welcomed by Hadji Mohammed's father and children. The elderly father told the family that his son had died from grief over the Armenians' fate and returned the family's valuables. They then began to sell these, one item at a time, at the local bazaars and were thereby able to survive for several months after their return. Mom always spoke admiringly of Hadji Mohammed and his father. She had fond memories of these kind and gentle Turks.

> During World War I, family losses were common among the warring countries, including the Turks. It wasn't unusual for families to lose 50% or more of its members. Death and suffering was widespread, so much so that the Armenian tragedy has become only a footnote in history, its significance lost.
>
> The Ottoman troika, Talaat, Jemal and Enver, took advantage of the war as a cover to implement a policy of genocide. Ironically, many Armenians had joined the Ottoman army when the war started but they were soon killed or reduced to slaves in labor camps. Despite many Armenians being hidden by friendly Turks, by war's end the estimated Armenian death toll came to 1.5 million from a little less than 2 million originally in the country. At the time, there were about 4 million Armenians worldwide.

While in Antioch, Mom learned to cook. She lived in a "havoush", a courtyard with several families sharing a common kitchen. This became her "culinary institute" where she learned to cook from several experienced "chefs"—Arab, Armenian, Greek and Turkish. The kind ladies found Mom to be an eager student and generously shared their skills and talents with her.

Mom had been living in Bitias for several years when Pop arrived home from the United States in 1924. Our parents met and married that same year. I was born in December of 1925, Anna in July, 1929. We lived in Bitias until 1939 when we found ourselves trapped by a fateful international decision.

After World War I, the League of Nations authorized a French mandate over Lebanon and Syria. Within Syria was the Sanjak of Alexandretta (Iskandarun) which included Antioch, Suedia and Musa Dagh. In 1939, when Europe was on the brink of another world war, the British signed a mutual assistance agreement with Turkey followed by the French who then abandoned the Sanjak to the Turks. The land transfer had a drastic effect on the Armenians there. If not for that, our family would be living in Bitias today.

Feeling threatened by the return of Turkish rule, the Armenians of Bitias, Yohun Oluk, Kheder Bey, Kabusia and Haji Habibli chose to leave Turkey. The remarkable survival of the Armenians of Musa Dagh during World War I had made them marked people, and the events of 1915 were still fresh in everyone's mind. Since they did not feel they could be free and safe under Turkish rule, they decided to abandon their homes. So in the summer of 1939, our family, along with thousands of Musa Daghtsis from five of the six villages and neighboring hamlets, left their ancestral lands. The majority of Armenians of Vakef stayed and today it remains the only Armenian village in all Turkey.

The French evacuated the Armenians of Musa Dagh. We were loaded in cargo trucks and dropped on the hot sands and open skies of Ras al Basit on the Mediterranean, where we lived for about forty days in makeshift huts. From there, we were taken by boat to Tripoli, transferred and taken in cattle cars to Riyak and then by truck to Anjar, all in Lebanon. There, in an open field, we settled.

Leaving behind our homes and our beloved mountain was a heart-wrenching decision and almost as devastating as the events of 1915. Most families could trace their ancestry in Suedia back centuries.

In Bitias, Mom perfected what she had learned in the common kitchen in

Antioch and, as we moved out of Turkey, she assimilated new recipes in all our subsequent homes for the next few decades. Mom remained a culinary student throughout her life and always tried new dishes and recipes.

I spent my life in schools and colleges, with books and with travel and ultimately became a history teacher. I avoided the kitchen. It was different for my sister Anna. She did not wait for the cooking baton to be passed to her. She caught it and ran. She watched Mom make the preparations of all these dishes, learning directly instead of from recipes, just as Mom had done in the common kitchen in Antioch. To this day she remains Mom's true disciple. Without recipes, she goes to the kitchen and produces one sumptuous feast after another, all made with ingredients and formulas residing entirely in her head. The rest of us sing her praises and enjoy every morsel.

Louisa, 17 years my junior, caught a baton of her own. Gradually, her attentions have gone more and more into cooking — all kinds of cooking. She married, started a family and has grown to love cooking and gardening. Because she has been away from home since college, she didn't have the opportunity to watch either Mom or Anna produce their Armenian dishes but she has, of course, learned a few by asking. At the same time she has also pursued a large range of worldly concoctions. At bedtime she reads recipes.

With this book, she gets something she has always wanted - the formulas to our homeland dishes as well as some of the stories I have written in the Epilogue. And, the baton can be passed on to Alex.

We confined the recipes in this book, with some exceptions, to those that are unique to Musa Dagh. Exceptions are those that were either slight variations or were impractical to omit. Some of our pilafs are unique so we included our recipe for standard pilaf as well. Of those we simply couldn't omit are tabouli, hummus, baba ghanoush, shish kebab and some dolmas and sarmas (which we call doolmos and sarmos). Richard says that Anna's shish kebab is better than any he's ever had.

The recipes are presented as follows:

English Name
Musa Daghtsi Name

Beverages

- Yogurts & Cheeses
- Breads
- Appetizers
- Salads
- Soups & Stews
- Vegetables
- Pilaf
- Stuffed Vegetables
- Meat Dishes
- Token Fish
- Pickles, Relish & Sauces
- Snacks
- Desserts

Demitasse Coffee
KAHFO

Demitasse coffee cups and a special pot called a jezvo can be purchased in Middle Eastern stores.

> 4 demitasse cups of water
> 2 teaspoons sugar
> 4 teaspoons demitasse coffee

1. Combine sugar and water in a demitasse pot on low heat. Stir until sugar dissolves.
2. Add coffee and stir several times.
3. Let coffee rise slowly allowing foam to form. Do not let it boil over.
4. Remove pot from heat and tap it twice. Pour about a spoonful of coffee in each cup, dividing the foam as evenly as possible.
5. Pour remaining coffee and fill up each cup. The double pouring helps distributes the foam evenly in each cup. A good hostess serves cups with the most foam to guests.

▸ *Serves four*

Yogurt Drink
AYROON OR TAN

Every Armenian knows how refreshing a cold glass of *tan* can be on a hot summer day. For Musa Daghtsis, however, the best *tan* is the by-product of churned yogurt for making butter.

Tan can be thick or thin, depending on one's taste. When thick, Mom called it "the poor man's tan." When watery, it was called "the rich man's tan." Mom's explanation was that, "a poor man probably gets all his nutrients from the yogurt so he adds very little water, whereas the rich man serves more people using less yogurt".

Poor Man's Tan*

    1 cup yogurt
    1 cup cold water

Beat yogurt well, add cold water and stir.

*Note: For "Rich Man's Tan," double the water to two cups or add water according to desired consistency.

BEVERAGES
Yogurts & Cheeses

BREADS
APPETIZERS
SALADS
SOUPS & STEWS
VEGETABLES
PILAF
STUFFED VEGETABLES
MEAT DISHES
TOKEN FISH
PICKLES, RELISH & SAUCES
SNACKS
DESSERTS

Yogurt
Madzon

In all our recipes, we use our homemade yogurt. Our "culture" has been in our family almost sixty years. We received our culture or starter from Mom's cousin Aunt Varter who had it in her family over twenty years. Legend has it that somewhere in the Middle East a shepherd made the first yogurt when he left his milk in a leather sack and, several hours later, discovered that the liquid had turned into a tasty solid mush. Many families have yogurt cultures that go back centuries.

We make a quart of yogurt at least three times a week. As experienced yogurt makers know, each new bowl provides a fresh source of culture for the next bowl. We have shared our culture with many friends who in turn have shared it with others.

Yogurt is a basic food for us. Besides enjoying it fresh, we use it as a sauce on meats or on steamed vegetables, such as spinach or chard. Often, it is the stock for soup.

Homemade Yogurt

    1 quart milk–whole, 2%, 1% or skim*
    1 tablespoon of yogurt culture or starter

1. Bring milk to a boil on low heat and let it rise slowly.
2. Pour milk into a glass bowl and set it on top of a towel large enough to wrap around the bowl.
3. Cool it to lukewarm, about 100° F. Add culture and stir once. Place a plate over the bowl and wrap the bowl in the towel.
4. Let it sit for 7-10 hours. Take care not to bump it.
5. Carefully move bowl into the refrigerator and refrigerate 4-5 hours. Be sure to save some culture for your next yogurt.

*Note: For the past several years, we have been making yogurt with skim milk. If using skim milk, stir the milk constantly while bringing it to a boil. Skim milk builds a thick film at the bottom of the pot if not stirred. Also, yogurt from skim milk will have some water on top. Spoon off the water before refrigeration.

Yogurt Cheese or Drained Yogurt
Kamoodz Madzon

>1 quart yogurt
>muslin cloth bag*

1. Pour a quart of homemade yogurt in a clean muslin-cloth bag and place it in a colander. Place the colander in a bowl and refrigerate overnight.
2. Spoon into a container for further use. Cover and refrigerate. It will keep for about a week.

Uses for *Kamoodz Madzon*: Mix with pepper paste to use as a spread on pita bread; add favorite herbs (oregano, summer savory) and olive oil and use it as a spread or dip; May use it for a substitute for sour cream or cream cheese for cooking or baking.

*Note: For small portions, it is possible to substitute paper towels (Bounty) for the bag.

▸ *Yields 2-3 cups of drained yogurt*

String Cheese
Kishoodz Bener

>5 pounds curd cheese
>black caraway seeds
>salt

1. Let cheese rest at room temperature for about two hours.
2. Preheat oven to 400° F.
3. Divide the curd evenly into five portions.
4. Place cheese on 10 inch diameter pizza pan lined with foil.
5. Cut cheese into 3x3 inch cubes. Slice each cube into ¼ inch thick slices.
6. Put pan in the oven for 2-3 minutes or until cheese is soft and malleable.
7. Remove cheese from the oven and immediately sprinkle with a pinch of caraway seeds. With a spoon gather the cheese and make two or three

separate balls.

8. Pick up one ball and make a hole in the center. Carefully stretch the cheese into a large circle or loop.
9. Fold the cheese and repeat stretching it until, as the cheese cools, it loses its elasticity. When the loop is about 8 inches long, twist the ends in opposite directions and form into a knot. The cheese may also be divided into three sections and braided.
10. Sprinkle cheese with salt and cool completely on a tray. Wrap individual pieces in plastic wrap and freeze.
11. As needed, thaw individual pieces in the refrigerator. Cut one end and pull cheese apart into strings and serve.

▸ *Makes ten knots or braids*

String Cheese

Ann's Cottage Cheese
CHEUKALUK

>1 cup whole milk
>1 quart plain homemade yogurt
>pinch of salt

1. Bring milk to a boil on low heat. Add yogurt, salt and stir well.
2. Cool. Drain in refrigerator through double layers of cheese cloth.
3. Seasonings may be added such as hot pepper flakes, hot pepper paste, summer savory and a few drops of olive oil.

Note: This is a good appetizer or snack when served on crackers or with pita bread.

▸ *Serves six to eight*

Ann's Cottage Cheese Spread
CHEUKALUK

>½ pound cottage cheese
>1 teaspoon tomato paste
>1 tablespoon pepper paste
>1 tablespoon olive oil
>summer savory flakes

Mix the first four ingredients, sprinkle with summer savory and serve with pita bread or crackers. This can be used for appetizer, light lunch, snack or breakfast.

▸ *Serves two*

Dried Cheese Balls
SOORKI

This recipe makes a cheese that tastes somewhat like a hot, blue cheese

2 cups farmer's cheese (*cheukaluk*)
2 tablespoons hot pepper paste
1 tablespoon summer savory flakes
1 teaspoon allspice
1 teaspoon cumin
salt to taste
1 tablespoon olive oil

1. Place a muslin cloth in a sieve and place it in a container that will hold the sieve. Pour the farmer's cheese (*cheukaluk*) into the sieve and let it drain in the refrigerator. This can take up to 24 hours depending on the amount of liquid in the cheese. Drained cheese should feel firm to the touch.
2. Transfer drained cheese to a mixing bowl and add the remaining ingredients. Mix well with hands.
3. Cover a shallow pan with several layers of paper towels. Pinch a chunk of the cheese mixture and shape it into a round ball (the amount should be between the size of a ping pong to tennis ball). Place it on the paper towels. Repeat for the remaining mixture. Refrigerate the cheese balls.
4. Within a few days, mold will form on the balls. Allow the mold to cover the balls completely. This process dries and hardens the cheese balls.
5. Use a paper towel and thoroughly wipe off the mold on each cheese ball. Take care to keep the balls from breaking.
6. Return the cheese balls to a clean pan covered with layers of paper towel. Refrigerate a second time for several days.
7. Wipe cheese balls again with paper towels. Place them in a jar and refrigerate. It will take several weeks for the cheese to dry thoroughly.
8. When ready to serve, dice *soorki* in a bowl. Add 1-2 teaspoons of extra virgin olive oil.

▸ *Serve with pita bread. Excellent appetizer.*

Beverages
Yogurts & Cheeses
Breads

Appetizers
Salads
Soups & Stews
Vegetables
Pilaf
Stuffed Vegetables
Meat Dishes
Token Fish
Pickles, Relish & Sauces
Snacks
Desserts

Breakfast Rolls
Choereg

¼ cup lukewarm water
1 cup + 2 teaspoons sugar
2 packets active dry yeast
1 cup warm milk
1 cup melted clarified butter (page 31)
4 eggs lightly beaten
6 cups all purpose flour
¼ cup sesame seeds

1. Proof yeast: Pour ¼ cup warm water into a tall glass. Add the two teaspoons sugar and stir until it dissolves. Add the yeast, stir gently and place in warm area. The yeast should bubble and foam within 15 minutes. If not, the yeast is not active and shouldn't be used.
2. In a bowl, combine the milk, butter and the remaining sugar. Add the eggs and mix well.
3. In a large bowl, combine the flour and the yeast and mix with a spoon. Add the milk mixture one third at a time. Blend flour well before each addition.
4. Knead for 15 minutes until dough is smooth. Form into a large ball and place in a bowl. Cover and let it rise in a warm area.
5. Preheat oven to 350° F. Pinch a small handful of dough about the size of a golf ball and roll it on a flat surface that has been sprinkled with sesame seeds. Roll until the dough

String cheese and choereg

forms a rope 7-8 inches long. The rope can be formed into different shapes. Double the rope and twist it once or form each rope into a knot. Arrange *choeregs* on an ungreased baking sheet and let them rise uncovered.
6. Bake until lightly golden brown. Cool and place them in zip lock bags in the refrigerator or freezer. Heat in oven before serving.

▸ *Makes three dozen choeregs*

Cheese Bread
Banderoom Hootz

Bread Dough
1 ½ packets active dry yeast
1 ½ teaspoons sugar
¼ cup warm water, plus additional warm water for later use
7 cups all-purpose flour
1 teaspoon salt

1. Proof yeast: Pour ¼ cup warm water into a tall glass. Add the 1 ½ teaspoons sugar and stir until it dissolves. Add the yeast, stir gently and place in warm area. The yeast should bubble and foam within 15 minutes. If not, the yeast is not active and shouldn't be used.
2. Place flour in a large bowl and add the salt. Make a well in the center, add the proofed yeast and enough warm water to blend the dough. Transfer the dough to a board and knead for 10-15 minutes. While kneading, dip hands in warm water to make a sticky dough.
3. Form into a large ball and place in a flat pan. Cover and let rise in a warm place.
4. After the dough rises, form four balls. Cover with a damp cloth and let the balls rise again in the pan. While dough is rising, prepare the topping.

Topping

1 dozen medium onions, diced
2-3 tablespoons hot pepper paste or to taste
½ cup blue cheese, crumbled
¾ cup grated Parmesan cheese

1 cup large-curd cottage cheese, thoroughly drained through double
   cheese cloth
2 tablespoons crushed dry summer savory
2 tablespoons olive oil, plus additional for later use

1. Preheat oven at 400° F.
2. Mix well all the above ingredients.
3. Lightly oil pizza pan with crisco and dust with flour. Place one ball of dough into the pan and spread it like a pizza.
4. Add one fourth of the topping, spreading it evenly.
5. Bake the bread 15-20 minutes until the bread is lightly brown.
6. Repeat the process from step three for the remaining three balls.
7. Let the flat breads cool completely and then slice them into eight triangles.
8. Dip fingers in olive oil and evenly pat the topping.
9. Refrigerate. Keeps up to one week.
10. If preferred warm, heat in oven before serving.

▸ *Makes four breads*

Flaky Coil Bread
BAGHASH

This bread is similar to a large flaky croissant.

   2 packets active dry yeast
   ¼ cup warm water
   2 eggs lightly beaten
   1 small can evaporated milk (5 fluid ounces)
   ¼ cup olive oil
   2 heaping teaspoons sugar
   9 cups all-purpose flour
   melted clarified butter (page 32)

1. Proof yeast: Pour ¼ cup warm water into a tall glass. Add the two teaspoons sugar and stir until it dissolves. Add the yeast, stir gently and place

The Recipes of Musa Dagh

in warm area. The yeast should bubble and foam within 15 minutes. If not, the yeast is not active and shouldn't be used.

2. In a small bowl, combine eggs, evaporated milk and olive oil.
3. Combine flour and sugar in a large bowl. Make a well in the center and add the yeast mixture, the milk mixture and a little warm water.
4. Knead dough, gradually adding warm water until dough does not stick to hands or bowl. Kneading time is approximately 10-15 minutes.
5. Form dough into a large ball and place it in a pan. Cover with a deep bowl and let it rise in a warm location.
6. Preheat oven at 350° F.
7. Divide dough into 10 small balls and place them in a pan with some space in between. Cover with a damp cloth and let dough rise a second time.
8. Sprinkle some flour on a flat working surface. Flatten one ball with your hands, sprinkle some flour and continue rolling the dough with a rolling pin or thin dowel until the dough is ¼ inch thick. Brush with clarified butter and cut dough into one inch width strips. Begin forming a spiral ball, attaching one strip to another. Continue the process for another ball attaching strips to form a round loaf. Use total of 2 ½ balls to form each loaf of round bread.
9. Place rolled bread in an ungreased pie plate and press gently to flatten bread. Cover with a wet cloth. Continue the process for the remaining balls. Let breads rise.

Baghash is excellent with Armenian string cheese and honey

10. Bake loaves until golden brown, about 25 minutes.
11. Serve with honey

Note: Wrap individual loaves tightly in aluminum foil to freeze for several months. Thaw in foil and heat before serving.

▸ *Makes four loaves*

Clarified Butter

1. Melt two pounds lightly salted butter over low heat. Skim off foamy surface and cool about ten minutes.
2. Gently pour butter into a jar and discard solids at the bottom. Refrigerated clarified butter will keep for several months.

Holiday Rings
Peegegh

Making *peegegh* is an oily process and rolling the dough while simultaneously keeping it moist makes an exercise in timing. This recipe makes about 36 *peegeghs* so you should roll out about six balls of dough at a time while keeping the rest under moist cover.

>   2 packets active dry yeast
>   2 ½ cups lukewarm water
>   ½ cup + 2 teaspoons sugar
>   8 cups flour
>   2 teaspoons cinnamon
>   2 teaspoons cloves
>   4 teaspoons fennel seeds
>   2 teaspoons black caraway seeds
>   1 cup olive oil

1. Proof yeast: Pour ¼ cup warm water into a tall glass. Add the two teaspoons sugar and stir until it dissolves. Add the yeast, stir gently and place in warm area. The yeast should bubble and foam within 15 minutes. If not, the yeast is not active and shouldn't be used.

The Recipes of Musa Dagh

2. In a large bowl combine the flour, the remaining sugar and all the spices. Mix well.
3. Make a well in the center of the flour mixture, add the yeast and a third cup of lukewarm water. Blend gradually with your hands and add the remaining water.
4. Transfer dough to a working surface and knead for 20 minutes, occasionally pounding the dough on the board. Dough is ready when it is smooth and does not stick to the board and fingers. Form into a ball and place it in a large bowl, cover and let rise to double its size.
5. Sprinkle a platter, or flat tray with flour. Pinch off some dough, about the size of a small egg. Roll it into a ball and place it on the platter leaving an inch between the balls. To cover the balls, place some narrow jars on and around the tray and cover with damp cloth, making a tent. This prevents the damp cloth from touching the dough. Let them rise to almost double in size. You may need more than one platter.
6. Gently remove one ball and place it on a well-floured board and roll it out with a dowel or rolling pin into a thin 12 to 15 inch circle. You may choose to make up to six circles at a time to minimize rolling with the oily hands that will follow.
7. Place a circle on a separate tray. Dip fingers in olive oil and sprinkle some on the circle spreading the oil evenly.
8. Pick up the edge of the circle and fold in one inch. Continue folding until the circle has become a one inch wide strip. Dip fork into olive oil and press the fork on the dough along its length. This process will flatten the folded dough and leave a lined design. Press the ends together to make a circle.
9. Place the *peegegh* on an ungreased baking sheet leaving space between the rings. Set the baking sheets, uncovered, in a warm area and let the *peegegh* rise.
10. Repeat steps 6-9 until all the balls of dough have been formed into *peegeghs*.
11. Bake at 350° F. until golden brown. Remove from oven, pat lightly with olive oil and place them in a large pot. Cover pot after the *peegegh* cools.

Note: *Peegegh* is labor intensive but worth the effort. We make it once or twice during the holidays. *Peegegh* goes well with feta cheese and honey. Freezes well wrapped in foil. Defrost in refrigerator and heat in oven before serving.

▸ *Makes about three dozen*

Cheese Boerek
BOEREK

1 pound curd cheese*
1 bunch Italian parsley, minced, spread on paper towels to drain
1 medium onion
1 cup clarified butter (page 32)
1 pound phyllo dough

1. Defrost cheese if frozen. Grate coarsely and place it on a tray covered with paper towels to drain all moisture. Both cheese and parsley must be dry.
2. Mince onion and cook with two tablespoons of clarified butter on low flame until onion wilts. Stir occasionally. Remove from heat.
3. Add cheese to onion and mix well. Add parsley and mix well.
4. Preheat oven to 400° F. Lightly butter a rectangular baking pan.
5. Separate phyllo into two equal piles and immediately cover them with a damp kitchen towel. Phyllo dries out quickly and will become brittle.

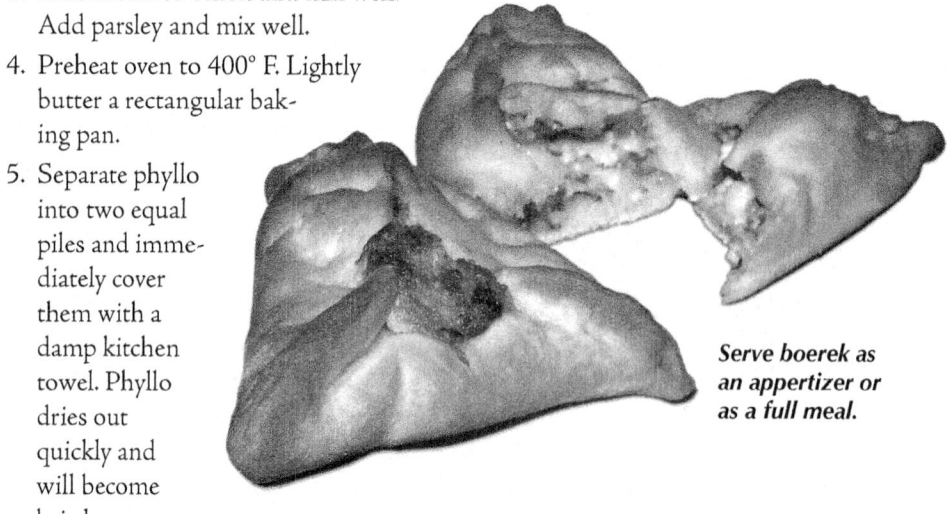

Serve boerek as an appertizer or as a full meal.

6. From the first pile of phyllo, place two pieces of dough on the prepared baking pan. Brush lightly with melted butter. Repeat until all the sheets from the pile are used.
7. Spread the cheese mixture evenly over the pile of dough.
8. Cover the cheese by repeating step six with the second pile.
9. Brush the top with butter and cut the dough into 2-2 ½ inch squares with a sharp knife.
10. Bake for 2-3 minutes. Immediately lower heat to 250° F. and bake until

golden brown about 20 minutes.

*Note: If curd cheese is unavailable in Middle Eastern stores, combine equal portions of cottage cheese and feta cheese. Drain and continue with directions.

▸ *Makes about 40*

Unleavened Flat Bread
SAJEH HOOTZ

> 6 ½ cups unbleached all purpose flour
> 1 teaspoon salt
> lukewarm water

1. Place flour and salt in a large bowl. Gradually add water while mixing with your hand. When the dough begins to form into a ball and pulls from the sides of the bowl, transfer the dough on a lightly floured board. Knead dough for about 15 minutes, occasionally pounding it on the board.
2. Pinch dough and form it into a 2 inch roll in diameter. Place it on a lightly floured pan. Continue forming dough into rolls. You will end with 30-35 rolls.
3. Cover with a damp towel topped with a plastic sheet. Let dough rest 2-3 hours.
4. Preheat oven 500° F. Lightly flour a board. Flatten one of the rolls and with hand. Sprinkle a little flour and, with a dowel, roll the dough from the center out as thin as possible. When the dough sticks to the dowel or board, sprinkle more flour. Continue rolling dough and form the flat bread into a 15 inch circle.
5. Transfer the flat bread on a round baking tray and gently place in the broiler section of the oven.
6. Bake for about one minute, turn over and bake the other side for an additional minute.
7. The baked bread will be firm and light brown. Once removed from the oven, cool bread completely and store in a cool area.

Bread will keep for several weeks. It can be eaten dry as chips or moistened for sandwich wraps. To soften bread, sprinkle each flat bread with water or hold it under cold water. Once wet, pile on top of each other, cover with a thick towel and let rest for several hours or overnight. Test, if necessary, sprinkle again with water.

*Note: This thin bread is excellent with kebabs, *pivaz*, cheese, honey, olives, yogurt.

▸ *Makes 30-35 flat breads*

BEVERAGES
YOGURTS & CHEESES
BREADS

Appetizers

SOUPS & STEWS
VEGETABLES
PILAF
STUFFED VEGETABLES
MEAT DISHES
TOKEN FISH
PICKLES, RELISH & SAUCES
SNACKS
DESSERTS

It's hard to imagine a cookbook of the Middle East without recipes for two popular dishes from the region—hummus and baba ghanoush. Mom did not make these dishes in Bitias but Louisa makes hummus and baba ghanoush all the time. We are including her versions of these recipes here.

Tabouli (page 42), cheese boerek (page 38), olives and stuffed grape leaves (page 90) may also be served as appetizers. On the other hand, we often serve hummus, with pita bread, as well as baba ghanoush and boerek as complete meals in themselves.

Hummus

1 can chick peas, drained and rinsed (15-16 ounces)
juice of one lemon
3-4 tablespoons of tahini paste
1 tablespoon cumin
2 cloves garlic (optional)
salt

1. Place all the ingredients in a food processor and blend until smooth. Add tablespoonfuls of warm water for desired consistency and texture.
2. Just before serving, garnish hummus with paprika, olive oil, and chopped parsley.
3. Serve with pita bread or sliced, raw vegetables

Note: For dry chick peas; soak 1 cup of dried chick peas over night. Rinse and add chick peas to boiling water. Simmer uncovered until soft, 30 to 45 minutes. Use same proportions of the remaining ingredients as above.

▸ *Serves four*

Baba Ghanoush

1 large roasted eggplant
juice of one lemon
⅓ cup tahini paste
1 tablespoon cumin
salt

1. Copy procedure for roasted eggplant.
2. Drain the bitter juices of eggplant in a colander for 15 minutes. The taste of baba ghanoush depends on the quality of the eggplant. Generally, light colored eggplant flesh tastes sweeter.
3. Place all the ingredients in a food processor and blend until smooth. Garnish with chopped black olives.
4. Serve with pita bread

Note: According to taste, adjustments can be made both to hummus and baba ghanoush by increasing or decreasing the basic ingredients--lemon juice, tahini paste and cumin. Cloves of garlic can be added as well.

▸ *Serves four*

Beverages
Yogurts & Cheeses
Breads
Appetizers

Salads

Soups & Stews
Vegetables
Pilaf
Stuffed Vegetables
Meat Dishes
Token Fish
Pickles, Relish & Sauces
Snacks
Desserts

Potato Salad
Kamoom Salato

1 medium onion, sliced lengthwise
1 teaspoon pepper paste
2 medium red potatoes, boiled, peeled and cut into bite-size pieces
1 medium red or green pepper, sliced lengthwise
1 medium tomato, cut into bite-size pieces
1 small bunch parsley, diced
juice of ½ lemon
2 tablespoons olive oil
salt to taste

1. In a serving bowl, gently knead onions and pepper paste.
2. Add the remaining ingredients and stir.

▸ Serves four

Fava Beans with Yogurt
Madznoom Paglo

1 pound fresh fava beans, washed, strings and ends removed and cut into bite-size pieces
5 cups water
2 cups plain yogurt*
salt to taste
dry mint flakes

1. Bring water to a boil. Add fava beans and simmer until beans are soft. This should take about 8-10 minutes.
2. Drain beans and cool. Beat yogurt lightly and add to beans.
3. Add salt and mix well. Sprinkle mint before serving.

*Note: May substitute lemon juice for yogurt. Salad makes a refreshing light lunch served with pita bread.

▸ Serves four

Red Kidney Bean Salad
Plakee 1

1 can light or dark red kidney beans (15.5 ounces)
1 tablespoon olive oil
¼ cup chopped parsley
1 small onion, minced

1. Bring beans to a boil on medium hear. Remove from heat and add olive oil.
2. Add lemon juice and stir.
3. Serve in individual bowls and add onions and parsley on top.

▸ *Serves two or three*

Red Bean Salad
Plakee 2

1 can of red kidney beans (15.5 ounces)
1 small onion, peeled and diced
1 small bunch parsley, washed, patted dry and chopped
1 tablespoon olive oil
cayenne pepper to taste
lemon slices

1. Bring beans to a boil on medium heat.
2. Remove from heat and add the next three ingredients. Mix well.
3. Serve with cayenne pepper and lemon slices.

▸ *Serves two*

Tabouli

This popular dish is now prepared by many cooks. Recipes vary with the amount and combination of vegetables and the preparation process.

¾ cup bulgur, #1

juice of ½ lemon
salt to taste
1 tablespoon tomato paste
1 tablespoon pepper paste
several fresh mint leaves or generous sprinkle of dry mint
1 medium ripe tomato, seeded, diced and drained—save juice
1 medium bell pepper, seeded
4 scallions, green and white parts
1 small cucumber, if seeds large—scoop out
1 large bunch fresh parsley—Italian more tasty
3-4 tablespoons olive oil

1. Place bulgur in a large bowl and add the next five ingredients and the tomato juice. Add enough cold water to cover bulgur.
2. While bulgur soaks for about 40 minutes, dice all the vegetables.
3. Taste bulgur mixture and adjust salt and lemon juice according to taste. If bulgur is still hard, add a little more cold water and mix.
4. Add diced vegetables and mix well.
5. Just before serving, add olive oil and stir gently.

▸ *Serves four*

Bulgur Salad with Cooked Vegetables
SUMUNDERGOOM PORTODJ

¾ cup #1 bulgur
1 teaspoon pepper paste
1 teaspoon tomato paste
salt to taste
¼ cup cold water
1 medium onion diced
¼ cup olive oil
1 small tomato, skinned, seeded, diced, drained—save juice
1 small bunch parsley, diced
1 small bell pepper, seeded, diced

1. Place bulgur in a large bowl and add the next four ingredients and the drained tomato juice. Soak for about half hour. Taste bulgur. If too dry, add a bit more water.
2. In the meantime, sauté onion in olive oil until onions are translucent. Add diced tomato and continue cooking for an additional 4-5 minutes.
3. Remove onion mixture from heat and add to bulgur. Let rest a few minutes.
4. Place on serving plate and arrange diced vegetables on top.

▸ Serves four

Garden Salad
BAKHCHEH SALATO

1 large tomato
2 small pickling cucumbers
1 bell pepper
3-4 scallions or
1 medium Vidalia or red onion
⅓ cup chopped parsley
1-2 tablespoons olive oil
fresh lemon juice to taste
salt to taste

1. Wash all the vegetables with cold water, drain, and pat dry.
2. Dice all the vegetables, place in a salad bowl and toss. Add olive oil, lemon juice, and salt and toss again. Serve immediately.

▸ Serves four

Yogurt with Eggplant
MADZNOODZ SIV BEDINJOON

1 large eggplant
1 cup plain yogurt
dry mint flakes
salt

1. Preheat oven to 400° F.
2. Make small slits in the eggplant and place on a baking pan covered with aluminum foil. Bake eggplant, turning it several times until soft.
3. Remove immediately and peal the outer skin. When cool, remove seeds and drain juices.
4. Cut eggplant into pieces. Do not mash. Refrigerate for half hour.
5. When cold, place eggplant in a bowl, add yogurt, salt and mix well. Sprinkle mint flakes before serving.

▸ *Serves four*

Watercress Salad
ARVAGAROOS

In Musa Dagh, watercress grew along our clean brooks running through the village. We harvested watercress growing near the springs among the pebbles.

    1 bunch watercress
    juice of ½ lemon
    1 tablespoon olive oil
    ¼ teaspoon hot pepper flakes
    salt to taste.

1. Wash watercress, pat dry and cut into 1 ½-2 inch pieces.
2. Add lemon juice, olive oil, pepper flakes, and salt.
3. Toss and serve.

▸ *Serves two or three*

Eggplant and Walnut Salad
SIV BEDINJNOOM SALATO

    1 large eggplant
    1 medium Vidalia or red onion
    ½ cup finely ground walnuts

1 green pepper
1 firm tomato
½ cup finely chopped parsley
fresh lemon juice to taste
salt to taste

1. Preheat oven to 400° F. Slit the eggplant in several places. Place it on a baking sheet covered with aluminum foil. Bake until soft, turning several times. Remove from oven and immediately peal off skin and drain juices. Cut a crisscross and refrigerate. Do not mash. This step can be done a day ahead.
2. Cut eggplant into small bite-size pieces and place it in a salad bowl.
3. Thinly slice onions lengthwise and place in bowl. Sprinkle salt and knead gently. Add to eggplant.
4. Add walnuts and mix well.
5. Wash and dry pepper and tomato. Cut into bite-size pieces and add to salad.
6. Add lemon juice and mix well. Taste for salt.
7. Sprinkle parsley on salad and serve immediately.

▸ *Serves four*

BEVERAGES
YOGURTS & CHEESES
BREADS
APPETIZERS
SALADS

Soups & Stews

VEGETABLES
PILAF
STUFFED VEGETABLES
MEAT DISHES
TOKEN FISH
PICKLES, RELISH & SAUCES
SNACKS
DESSERTS

Cooked Skinless Whole Wheat
Dzeedzoods Tseerin

Our recipes use uncooked skinless whole wheat unless specified. Since this wheat takes a long time to cook, we usually cook enough for several dishes and freeze for future use.

This wheat is usually found in Middle Eastern grocery stores.

1. Rinse 1 cup skinless whole wheat in cold water several times.
2. Place in a saucepan with 4 ½ cups of cold water. Bring to boil and simmer uncovered, without stirring, until water is absorbed, about an hour.
3. Remove from heat. Cool and freeze into individual portions for future meals.
4. Thaw and use in Soup de Paris, *Katmo*, etc. Check index for recipes.

Cabbage Soup or Soup de Paris
Turkhanoom Shoorbo

The language spoken in Bitias was an Armenian dialect called Kistinik. The natives also studied and spoke standard Armenian, the language spoken by Armenians almost everywhere.

One summer day, several Armenian college men from Aleppo, sought to escape their crowded city and remembered their classmate living in the small town of Bitias. They set out to find the home of their friend. The young man of Bitias was delighted at the arrival of his unexpected guests..

The guests enjoyed the hospitality and the tasty treats at their classmate's home as they conversed in Armenian. His aunt lived in his home during the summer months and had learned French as the cook at the French Consulate in Aleppo during the winter months and she invited the guests to stay for dinner. The son, knowing that they were only having a simple, cabbage soup, admonished her in Kistinik about serving peasant fare to sophisticated city folks. She assured him not to worry.

While the friends caught up on news, she prepared the meal. She set the table with her fine china and added olives, tonir bread and a large soup tureen. She invited the guests to the table and announced, "I'm delighted you came because I had planned to make the French Consulate's favorite, 'Soup de Paris.'"

The guests ate and ate and emptied the tureen, complimenting her with every spoonful. She had, in fact, served nothing more than the cabbage soup that was commonly cooked throughout the village.

The story quickly spread through Bitias and cabbage soup acquired the new name of "Soup de Paris". Here it is.

⅓ cup cooked skinless whole wheat (page 48)
2 cups water
1 small cabbage—remove stem and cut leaves into bite-size pieces
1 small zucchini (optional) cut into bite-size pieces
1 medium onion, diced
¼ cup olive oil
1 medium egg
1 quart yogurt
salt to taste

1. Use a saucepan large enough to hold all the ingredients. Bring water and skinless whole wheat to a boil. Simmer uncovered on low heat until soft. Don't stir. If necessary, add spoonfuls of hot water.
2. Add zucchini and cabbage and cook uncovered 15 more minutes. Add salt, stir, and remove from heat.
3. While soup cooks, sauté onions in olive oil until light brown. Add to soup.
4. In a separate saucepan, place the yogurt and egg on low heat and stir constantly. This prevents the yogurt from curdling. Bring close to a boil. Add to soup.

▸ Serves six

Split Red Lentil Soup
MULKHATOOM SHOORBO

1 cup water
¼ cup rice
¾ cup red lentils

4 cups boiling water
2 medium onions, halved and sliced lengthwise
¼ cup olive oil
salt to taste

1. Place the first three ingredients in a saucepan and bring to boil. Continue cooking on medium heat and stirring constantly. Periodically add warm water until the mixture is cooked well. The amount of water will determine the consistency of the soup. Add salt to taste.
2. While the soup is cooking, sauté onions in olive oil until the onions are translucent and turned light brown.
3. Remove soup from heat and add onions.

▸ *Serves four*

Lentil Soup Variation with Cayenne
HAMIMOOM MULKHATOOM SHOORBO

This substitutes either whole wheat or barley for rice in the previous lentil soup recipe. In Kistinik, *hamimoom* means pepper.

¼ cup cooked skinless whole wheat (page 48)
or ¼ cup cooked barley; follow same preparation on page 48
cayenne pepper to taste

1. Follow recipe for *Mulkhatoom Shoorbo* through step 1, but substitute cooked skinless whole wheat or barley for rice. Add cayenne pepper according to taste.
2. Continue with steps 2 and 3 of *Mulkhatoom Shoorbo*.

▸ *Serves four*

Galagacia Soup
GOOLOOGOOS

Galagacia is found in Latin markets. It resembles sweet potatoes but with a very dark skin.

> 2 pounds *gooloogoos*
> juice of one lemon
> ¼ pound lean lamb, cubed
> 5 cups water
> ¼ cup chick peas, soaked overnight and cooked until soft—drain
> 1 quart plain yogurt
> one egg
> salt to taste

1. Peel *gooloogoos*, cut into bite-size pieces, add lemon juice, and set aside for about 45 minutes.
2. Bring lamb and one cup of water to a boil and cook for five minutes. Drain. Wash meat and saucepan. Return meat to saucepan with four cups of water. Bring to a boil and simmer covered until meat is tender.
3. Add chick peas. Drain *gooloogoos*, add to mixture and cook about 20 minutes until *gooloogoos* is soft.
4. While soup cooks, prepare yogurt. In a separate saucepan, mix the egg with yogurt and place it on low heat, stirring constantly until yogurt is hot. Do not boil. Add to soup. Taste for salt. If a thinner soup is preferred, add some hot water accordingly.

Note: Excellent with bulgur pilaf

▸ *Serves six*

White Bean Soup
Leyvasoom Tutteh Cheur

> 1 cup Great Northern white beans soaked overnight in cold water
> ½ pound lean lamb cubes
> 1 medium onion, sliced lengthwise
> 4 cups water
> 1 tablespoon tomato paste
> juice of ½ lemon

1 ½ tablespoons butter
salt to taste

1. Wash beans in cold water. Cover with water and cook slowly until soft.
2. In a saucepan, add enough water to cover meat cubes. Bring to a boil and cook five minutes. Remove meat and wash with cold water. May save broth for soup.
3. Wash saucepan. Add meat and ½ cup cold water and bring to a boil. Simmer uncovered until all the water is absorbed.
4. Add butter and onions and cook until onions are soft.
5. Add the remaining water and the rest of the ingredients and cook until water begins to simmer. Add salt and lemon juice to taste.
6. Cook uncovered for five minutes. Let rest five minutes, covered, before serving.

▸ *Serves four*

Potato Multi-Bean Soup
KAMOOM TUTTEH CHEUR

¼ cup chick peas
¼ cup white (navy or cannellini) beans
½ cup red kidney beans
4-5 cups water
¼ cup lentils
1 medium red potato, cut bite size
1 tablespoon tomato paste
juice of half lemon
¼ cup olive oil
1 medium onion, coarsely chopped
3-4 cloves garlic, peeled and halved
salt to taste
large pinch of dry mint

1. Soak the first three ingredients overnight. Drain and place them in saucepan with two cups of water and boil. Simmer for 10 minutes uncovered.

Add one cup of cold water and continue cooking.
2. When the beans are half done, wash lentils and add along with another cup of cold water. Bring to a boil and cook for five minutes.
3. Add the next three ingredients and some salt. Cook until the potatoes are done.
4. Sauté onions and garlic in olive oil while soup is cooking. When soft and translucent, add them to the soup.
5. Add salt to taste. Mint may be sprinkled in individual bowls.

Note: According to desired soup consistency, boiling water may be added before step 4.

▶ *Serves six*

Swiss Chard with Multi-Bean Soup
ZULKHOOM TUTTEH CHEUR

¼ cup of each – dry chick peas, white beans, red beans
¼ cup coarse #3 bulgur
2-3 cups cold water
⅓ cup green lentils
1 bunch Swiss chard, about one pound
1 medium onion
¼ cup olive oil
1 tablespoon tomato paste
salt to taste
fresh lemon juice

1. Wash chick peas and beans with cold water. Place in a bowl, cover with cold water, and soak overnight.
2. Rinse the soaked legumes and place in a pot. Add cold water, bulgur, salt and cook over medium heat uncovered about 15-20 minutes.
3. Rinse lentils and add to legumes. Continue cooking additional 15-20 minutes.
4. Wash chard in cold water, drain, chop,* and add to pot. Continue cooking for 10 more minutes.

5. Add tomato paste, lemon juice and salt to taste. If a thinner soup is preferred, add more hot water at this time.
6. While soup is cooking, sauté thinly sliced onions in olive oil until lightly brown.
7. Add sautéed onions to soup and stir.

*Note: The white stems of the chard may be cut into small pieces and added to the soup or saved for another use.

▸ *Serves six*

Tomato Soup
BANADOOROOM SHOORBO

    1 quart broth, lamb or beef
    3 medium ripe tomatoes, peeled, seeded and diced
    ¼ cup thin noodles or ¼ cup cooked rice
    1 teaspoon tomato paste
    1 small bunch parsley, washed, patted dry and chopped
    fresh lemon juice to taste
    salt to taste

1. Bring broth to a boil, reduce heat and let simmer for few minutes.
2. Add noodles (or rice), tomatoes and tomato paste and continue cooking 5-8 minutes. Noodles will be soft.
3. Remove from heat, add salt, lemon juice and parsley. Stir and serve.

▸ *Serves four*

Vegetable Soup

    ½ pound lean lamb cubes
    5 cups water
    ¼ cup barley or skinless whole wheat
    1 large carrot
    1 medium potato

>   2 stalks celery with leaves
>   1 tablespoon tomato paste
>   juice of half lemon
>   salt to taste

1. Place meat in a pot with two cups water and bring to a boil uncovered. Boil about two minutes. Drain meat in colander. Rinse meat in cold water and wash the pot.
2. Return meat to pot and add two cups of water and skinless whole wheat or barley. Cook uncovered on medium heat until wheat/barley is soft about 20 minutes.
3. While meat and wheat/barley mixture cooks, wash and scrape the carrot and dice into small cubes, about the size of chick peas.
4. Wash and dice the celery about the same size, including the leaves.
5. Peal potatoes and cut into small cubes, about the same size as other vegetables.
6. Add all the diced vegetables and cook about 10-12 minutes.
7. Add tomato paste, lemon juice, and salt. A cup of hot water may be added at this stage if a thinner soup is desired. Continue cooking, uncovered on low heat until all the vegetables are done to desired softness.

Note: Half a cup of mixed chick peas and white beans may be added to this soup. Follow procedure for soaking dry beans in Swiss chard soup. The legumes may be added during step 2 of the preparation.

▸ *Serves four*

Head and Tongue Soup
Kelleh Patcha

This dish is popular in the Middle East. For us, the head *(kelleh)* of a young goat was the main ingredient and preparing it was a major operation.

This soup is unique! Its wonderful taste made it a prized favorite in Musa Dagh. With the unusual steps for preparation, it's not very likely this soup would be commonly served for a supper. You might not want to describe the preparation to your invited guests. Or do as Julia Child might have done. Assemble a group of intrepid guests with adventurous taste buds. Bon Apetit!

    1 goat's or lamb's head freshly severed
    1 cup of cooked chick peas
    cayenne pepper to taste
    garlic cloves to taste
    lemon juice to taste

The tongue and head are prepared separately but simultaneously

1. Cut the tongue out of the head and place it with several cups of water into pot and bring to a boil over medium heat. Lower heat and simmer for 10 minutes. Remove the tongue and scrape the outer layer with a knife. Wash tongue with cold water.
2. Put head on hot coals. Rotate and turn until the skin is totally charred.
3. Remove skin and hair, then wash the skull with cold water and place it in a large pot. Add the tongue and fill pot with water.
4. Bring to a boil, lower heat and let simmer for hours until meat begins to separate from bones and the tongue is soft. If necessary, add more boiling water to keep ingredients covered.
5. Remove head and tongue from the pot. Separate meat from bones, and cut meat into small morsels and return to pot. Discard bones.
6. Add the chick peas, cayenne pepper and more hot water if needed.
7. Adjust for salt and bring to a boil.
8. Remove pot from heat, add a healthy amount of crushed garlic and fresh lemon juice.

Note: Legend has it that in olden times, the simmering process went on all night and the *kelleh patcha* was declared ready with the first crow of the neighbor's rooster.

▸ *Serve hot to friends and neighbors.*

Tongue and Tripe Soup
PATCHA

We never had *kelleh patcha* in the United States. However, Mom concocted this recipe using a few tongues and a tripe which captured the flavor of our love for this soup minus a slight charred flavor.

> 1 lamb tripe, blanched
> 1 cup vinegar
> 3-4 small lamb tongues, blanched
> ½ cup chick peas, soak overnight in cold water
> 3-4 large cloves of garlic, peeled and crushed
> cayenne pepper flakes to taste
> fresh lemon juice
> salt

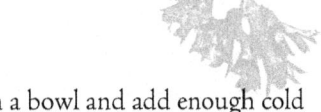

1. Blanch tripe. Wash tripe in cold water. Place in a bowl and add enough cold water to cover. Add vinegar and refrigerate overnight.
2. Remove tripe and discard water-vinegar solution. Wash tripe in cold water. Place it in a pot, adding fresh cups of water, cover, and bring to a boil. Lower heat and simmer for 10 minutes.
3. Remove tripe from boiling water, transfer to a cutting board, and scrape both sides well with a knife. Wash again with cold water and cut into bite-size pieces. Set aside.
4. Blanch tongues following steps 2 and 3 for tripe, except do not cut into pieces.
5. Place tongues and tripe in a large pot. Add several cups of water and bring to a boil. Cover and simmer for several hours, adding more hot water as needed.
6. Add chick peas. Add cayenne pepper to taste and continue cooking until meat and chick peas are soft. Adjust for salt.
7. Remove tongue from pot and cut into small morsels and return to pot and slowly bring to a boil.
8. Remove from heat. Add lemon juice and crushed garlic to taste.

▸ *Serves six*

SOUPS WITH DUMPLINGS

Yogurt soup and tomato soup can be served with or without bulgur-meat dumplings called *kaloors*. However, dough dumplings, called *agantch*, are only used in yogurt soup (all these recipes follow).

Yogurt Soup
Madznoom Shoorbo

>3-4 cups water
>1 quart plain yogurt
>1 egg
>salt to taste
>dry mint flakes

1. Bring water to a boil in a saucepan.
2. In a separate saucepan, bring yogurt and egg up to a boil on low heat, stirring constantly. Remove from heat and add to boiling water. Add salt and stir well. Sprinkle mint in individual bowls.

Note: some prefer to add boiled rice to this soup.

▸ *Serves four*

Dumplings: for Yogurt Soup
Agantch

Both dough and filling *(kima)* may be prepared ahead of time.

Dough: made without yeast

>2 ½ cups all purpose flour
>½ teaspoon salt
>lukewarm water to form dough

1. Mix flour and salt and gradually add water to form into dough. Knead well at least for ten minutes and divide into four balls.
2. Place balls on a floured tray and cover with cloth. Place cloth across several tall glasses to keep it from touching the dough. Add plastic sheet over cloth and let dough rest 5-6 hours.

Filling for *agantch* (kima)

    1 pound ground meat, preferably lamb
    ½ cup water
    1 tablespoon butter
    1 medium onion, diced
    1 teaspoon salt
    black and cayenne pepper to taste

1. In a large saucepan, cook meat and water on low heat, stirring occasionally.
2. When water evaporates, add butter and the remaining ingredients. Continue cooking, stirring frequently, until onions are soft. Remove from heat and let cool.

Assembling the *agantch*

1. Place one ball on a floured surface and sprinkle flour on a rolling pin. Roll dough into a thin sheet, adding additional flour if dough is sticky.
2. Cut dough with a sharp knife into 1 ½ inch squares. Place about one teaspoon filling in the center, fold diagonally and press dough over filling to form a triangle. Bring together the opposite two edges and press to form into a dumpling. Arrange dumplings on a floured tray. Finish forming dumplings with the remaining dough.

Cooking the *agantch*

1. Bring 6-8 cups of water to a gentle boil.
2. Place about a dozen *agantch* in a strainer and hold the strainer in the boiling water while *agantch* cooks for 4-5 minutes.
3. Remove cooked *agantch* and place it in a single layer on a large platter.
4. Repeat until all the *agantch* is cooked.

Serving the *agantch*.

Place several *agantch* in individual soup bowls, add yogurt soup.

▸ *Serves six*

Dumplings for Soups
Kaloor

Note: For the dumpling filling *(kima)*, you can use either the filling below or the keufteh meat filling found in the Meat Dishes section (page 110).

Dumpling filling (referred to below as "filling"): This can be prepared ahead of time.

   small bunch parsley, washed patted dry and minced
   ½ cup walnuts, chopped fine in a food processor
   2 tablespoon of butter
   1 teaspoon pepper paste or cayenne (optional)
   salt to taste

Mix the filling ingredients and set aside.

Keufteh Bulgur-meat Shell Mixture (referred to below as "shell mixture"): This cannot be made ahead of time. A food processor can be used for kneading bulgur-meat shell mixture.

   2 cups #1 bulgur
   1 pound lean leg of lamb – remove all fat and grind meat three times
   2 cups cold water and 4-6 ice cubes
   1 ½ tablespoons hot pepper paste
   1 teaspoon cumin
   salt to taste

1. Add enough cold water to thoroughly moisten bulgur and let soak for 15 minutes.
2. Using cold water with ice cubes, wet hands and knead bulgur for 10 minutes.
3. Add ⅔ of the meat, pepper paste, cumin, and salt. Using the iced water to keep your hands moist, knead for another 10 minutes. The **shell mixture** will become soft and pliable.
4. Halfway through using the **shell mixture**, it will need additional kneading,

so add the remaining ⅓ of the meat, sprinkle with cold water and knead 4-5 minutes.

Making the dumplings *(kaloors)*

Kaloors for soups are formed round and hollow, about the size of ping-pong balls and then filled. There should be space between the filling and shell. This allows the *kaloor* to float in the soup.

1. Take several pieces from the bulgur-meat **shell mixture**, each smaller than a ping pong ball, and set aside. Leave remaining mixture uncovered.
2. Roll a piece between the palms to form it into a round ball. It is critical to keep hands and fingers moist between steps 3-5.
3. Cradle the ball in the palm of one hand and gently poke a hole in the ball using the index finger of the other hand. Rotate and press mixture to form a shell, taking great care to keep the shell intact. The hollowed shell should be thin.
4. Put a teaspoon of **filling** in the shell. Seal the opening so that there is space around the **filling** in the shell.
5. Place the dumpling on an ungreased platter and continue forming shells until the **filling** and **shell mixtures** are finished.
6. Add *kaloors* to yogurt soup or tomato soup (recipes below) and cook for about 10 minutes at a gentle simmer.

▸ *Makes one to two dozen dumplings depending on size*

Kalooreugs

1. With the leftover **shell mixture**, rotate small portions of the mixture between palms forming balls the size of marbles.
2. Add *kalooreugs* to soup and cook for about 3-4 minutes at gentle simmer.

Yogurt Soup with Bulgur-meat Dumplings
MADZNOOM KALOOREUG

1. Prepare dumplings *(kaloors)* for the soup.
2. Bring yogurt soup (recipe above) to a boil. Gently place *kaloors* in the soup,

no more than 6-8 dumplings at a time, and cook for 10 minutes. With a spatula or a slotted spoon, transfer dumplings to a platter. Repeat until all the dumplings are cooked.
3. If using *kalooreugs* instead of *kaloors*, add as many *kalooreugs* as fit in the pot at a time and cook for 3-4 minutes. Remove and repeat until all *kalooreugs* are cooked.
4. When serving, place 3-4 dumplings or 5-6 *kalooreugs* in individual soup bowls then add yogurt soup.

▸ *Serves five to six*

Tomato Soup with Dumplings
BANADOOROOM KALOOR SHOORBO

¼ cup chick peas, soaked in cold water over night
1 tablespoon tomato paste

Stuffed dumplings (kuloor) being added to tomato soup

    5 cups broth, preferable lamb, may use beef broth
    lemon juice and salt to taste
    dry mint flakes

1. Prepare dumplings *(kaloors)* for the soup (page 60).
2. Cook chick peas until soft. Drain and set aside.
3. Bring broth to a gentle boil in a large soup pot. Add tomato paste, chick peas, lemon juice and salt.
4. For cooking and serving, follow steps 2-4 in the yogurt soup with bulgur-meat dumplings recipe above.

Note: Cooking several bones with meat in the soup makes this recipe even more flavorful.

▸ *Serves five or six*

Cold Soups

Yogurt Soup with Skinless Whole Wheat
Katmo 1

    1 cup pre-cooked skinless whole wheat (page 48)
    1 cup plain yogurt
    ½ cup cold water
    salt to taste

1. Place pre-cooked skinless whole wheat in a bowl.
2. Beat yogurt well, add water and salt. Mix well and pour over wheat. Stir and serve.

▸ *Serves two*

Yogurt Lentil Pilaf Soup
Katmo 2

    1 cup leftover Mujaddarah (see Pilaf section)

1 cup plain yogurt
½ cup cold water
salt to taste

1. Follow steps 1 and 2 of Katmo 1 above.

▶ Serves two

Cucumber Soup
JAJUGH

1 cup plain yogurt
1 ½ cups cold water for soup
1 cucumber
salt to taste
dry mint flakes
crushed garlic (optional)

1. Beat yogurt well. Add water and stir. Add crushed garlic, if using.
2. Peel cucumber, cut in half lengthwise and then into thin slices.
3. Add cucumber, salt, mint to yogurt and stir.

▶ Serves two

STEWS

Green Bean, Potato and Zucchini Stew
LEYVASOOM KAMA

3 tablespoons olive oil
1 medium onion, chopped
4-5 garlic cloves, peeled and halved
¾ pound green beans, ends trimmed and cut into 1 ½ inch pieces
1 ¼ cups boiling water
1 medium red potato, peeled and cut into bite-size pieces

1 small zucchini, washed and cut into bite-size pieces
1 medium tomato, skinned, seeded and diced
1 teaspoon tomato paste
salt to taste

1. In medium size saucepan, sauté onion and garlic in olive oil until soft and translucent.
2. Add beans and cook for five minutes, stirring several times.
3. Add the boiling water and the remaining ingredients. Cover and simmer about 20 minutes until vegetables are slightly soft.

▸ *Serves six*

Yogurt, Zucchini and Meat Stew
BOOREHNI

2 ½ cups cold water
½ pound cubed meat, preferably lamb
¼ cup chick peas, soaked in cold water overnight
2 medium zucchini, wash, and cut into bite-size pieces
2-3 cloves garlic, quartered
2 cups plain yogurt
1 egg white
salt to taste

1. Bring two cups of water and meat to boil in a saucepan. Simmer uncovered for five minutes. Drain and wash meat in cold water and wash saucepan also.
2. Return meat and half cup of water to saucepan and bring to a boil. Simmer covered for five minutes. Add chick peas and continue to simmer until both ingredients are slightly soft. Add a pinch of salt and warm water if necessary.
3. Stir in zucchini, add garlic and cook 10-12 minutes.
4. While stew is simmering, place yogurt with egg white in a separate saucepan.
5. Cook on low heat, stirring constantly until yogurt comes to a boil.

6. Add yogurt to stew and salt to taste.

▸ *Serves four*

Okra Stew
BAMIA

¼ pound cubed meat, preferably lamb
4 cups cold water
1 medium onion, peeled and coarsely chopped
1 tablespoon butter
2 ripe medium tomatoes, peeled, seeded and chopped
juice of one lemon
1 teaspoon tomato paste
½ pound small okra
salt to taste

1. In a medium saucepan, bring the meat to a boil in two cups of water and simmer for five minutes. Drain. Wash the meat in cold water and rinse the saucepan.
2. Return meat to saucepan adding half a cup of cold water. Bring to a boil and simmer until the water is absorbed.
3. Add butter and chopped onions and cook until onions are translucent.
4. Add 1½ cups of water, chopped tomatoes, tomato paste, lemon juice and salt. Cover and cook on low heat 15-20 minutes.
5. Gently stir in okra. Cover and cook 15 more minutes on moderate heat. It is done when okra is soft and has changed color.

▸ *Serves four*

Multi-Legume Stew
PUDT-PUDT

⅓ cup dry of each: red kidney beans, white beans (navy or kidney), dry chick peas
½ cup bulgur #3

2 cups cold water
¼ cup green lentils, rinsed
1 tablespoon tomato paste
salt to taste
1 medium onion, thinly sliced lengthwise
¼ cup olive oil

1. Soak the dry legumes overnight. Drain and rinse.
2. Place soaked legumes and bulgur in saucepan with cold water. Bring to a boil and simmer uncovered for about one hour.
3. Add lentils, salt, tomato paste and about another ¼ cup water and continue cooking 30 minutes longer.
4. While stew is cooking, sauté onions in olive oil until translucent.
5. Once water is absorbed, remove from heat and add olive oil with sautéed onions.
6. Let stew rest for ten minutes.

▸ *Serves four*

Chick Peas with Eggplant
Ciciroom Siv Bedinjoon

½ cup dry chick peas
1 medium eggplant
2 medium tomatoes
½ bell pepper
1 teaspoon tomato paste
1 small onion, diced
3 garlic cloves, halved
2 teaspoons olive oil
½ teaspoon butter
salt, water

1. Wash chick peas and soak overnight
2. Drain chick peas and wash again with cold water and place in a pot. Add ½ cup water, bring to a boil and simmer uncovered until peas are soft.

3. Wash and cut eggplant into bite-size pieces.
4. Seed and cut pepper into bite-size pieces.
5. Dip tomatoes in hot water, peal, remove seeds and chop.
6. Add vegetables and tomato paste to chick peas and ½ cup water. Cook for 20 minutes.
7. In a separate pan, melt butter with olive oil and sauté onion and garlic until lightly brown.
8. Add salt and sautéed onion/garlic and cook an additional five minutes.

▸ Serves four

Eggplant with Meat
MOOTFUNEH

⅓ pound cubed meat, preferably lamb
2-2 ½ cups water
2 medium tomatoes
½ bell pepper
1 medium size eggplant
hot pepper flakes
1 teaspoon tomato paste
fresh lemon juice to taste
salt

1. In a large pot, bring meat and 1 ½ cups of water to a boil. Let boil for one minute. Empty contents in a colander and rinse meat with cold water.
2. Wash pot and return meat and ½ cup cold water. Bring to a boil and cook meat until tender and all the water evaporates.
3. Dip tomatoes in hot water. Peal, seed and chop.
4. Seed pepper and cut into bite-size pieces.
5. Wash eggplant and cut into bite-size pieces. Add vegetables to meat mixture.
6. Add ¼ cup cold water, lemon juice, tomato paste, and pepper flakes.
7. Cook on medium heat for 15-20 minutes until eggplant is soft. Add more lemon juice or salt if needed.

▸ Serves four

Meat with Green Beans
MUSSOOM LEYVOOS

½ pound lean ground meat, preferably lamb
2 tablespoons olive oil
1 medium onion
1 pound green beans, washed and cut into bite-size pieces
2 medium tomatoes
1 teaspoon tomato paste
1 cup + 4 tablespoons water
salt

1. Place meat and 4 tablespoons of water in a pot and cook on low heat until all the water is absorbed. Add olive oil.
2. Cut onion into small squares, add to meat, and continue cooking on low heat. Cook until onion is translucent, stirring occasionally. Add beans.
3. Peel, seed and cut tomatoes and add to meat mixture. Add one cup water, adjust salt and cook additional 20-30 minutes.

▸*Serves four*

BEVERAGES
YOGURTS & CHEESES
BREADS
APPETIZERS
SALADS
SOUPS & STEWS

Vegetables

PILAF
STUFFED VEGETABLES
MEAT DISHES
TOKEN FISH
PICKLES, RELISH & SAUCES
SNACKS
DESSERTS

Potatoes

Potatoes with Sautéed Onions
Hubuloodz Kama

>   3 medium red potatoes
>   3 medium onions, halved and cut lengthwise in thin slices and sprinkled with salt
>   2 tablespoons olive oil
>   1 medium tomato, skinned, seeded and chopped
>   1 teaspoon tomato paste
>   salt to taste
>   black pepper and allspice mixture – ½ teaspoon of each

1. Boil potatoes and cool. Peel and slice into circular pieces of ¼ inch thickness.
2. Cook onions in olive oil until soft and translucent.
3. Add tomato and tomato paste and simmer until all the water is absorbed. Cool.
4. Spread onion-tomato mixture on a flat serving dish. Arrange potato slices on top and sprinkle spice mixture.
5. Serve room temperature.

▸ *Serves four*

Potato with Bulgur
Kamoom Portodj

>   2 medium red potatoes
>   1 cup bulgur – #1
>   ¼ cup olive oil
>   1 medium onion
>   1 teaspoon pepper paste
>   1 small bunch parsley washed, dried, and chopped
>   1 medium red or green pepper, diced into ¼ inch pieces

salt to taste

1. Boil potatoes until soft. Cool, peel and mash roughly with a fork.
2. Place bulgur in a bowl, add salt and enough cold water to cover. Let it sit for about ten minutes until the water is absorbed.
3. While bulgur soaks, sauté onion in olive oil. Let cool.
4. Mix bulgur with hands and add pepper paste. Continue mixing until bulgur begins to cling together. Add tablespoons of water if necessary.
5. Add mashed potatoes and mix it completely with the bulgur.
6. Stir in sautéed onions and add salt to taste.
7. Arrange potato-bulgur in a serving dish and spread parsley and peppers on top.

▸ *Serves four*

Potato with Skinless Whole Wheat
Kamoom Dzeedzoods Tseerin

1 cup skinless whole wheat
4-5 cups cold water
2 medium red potatoes, washed, peeled and cut into bite-size pieces
1 tablespoon tomato paste
2 tablespoons melted butter
salt to taste

1. Wash skinless whole wheat in cold water and drain.
2. Bring wheat and 4-5 cups of water to a boil. Cover and simmer until soft, about 45 minutes. Do not stir.
3. Add potatoes, tomato paste, salt and continue cooking until water is absorbed.
4. Add hot melted butter and stir.

▸ *Serves four*

OTHER VEGETABLES

Spinach with Onions
DABGUDOODZ SPANAKH

>1 bunch fresh spinach, washed well and cut to pieces
>or 1 box frozen chopped spinach, thawed and well drained. Omit step 1 when using frozen spinach.
>4-5 cups water
>1 medium onion, diced
>3 tablespoons olive oil
>1 cup plain yogurt

1. Bring water to a boil. Add fresh spinach and let it wilt about two minutes. Drain quickly under cold water. Squeeze out excess water.
2. In a saucepan, sauté onion in olive oil until soft. Add drained spinach and mix well.
3. Place on a serving dish and pour yogurt on top. This dish may be served hot or cold.

▸ *Serves four*

Mixed Beans with Walnuts
SEUD HEERISEH

>⅓ cup each of red beans and chick peas, soaked overnight in cold water
>¼ cup skinless whole wheat
>4-5 cups cold water
>1 cup walnuts ground to a paste
>salt and cayenne pepper to taste

1. Wash soaked beans and chick peas in cold water. Drain and place in a pot with the cold water.
2. Wash uncooked skinless whole wheat in cold water and drain. Add to beans and chick peas.

3. Add cayenne pepper and bring to a boil on medium heat. Simmer on very low heat until water is absorbed. Do not stir.
4. Add walnuts, salt and stir.

▶ *Serves four*

Fava Beans with Onions
HUBULOODZ PAGLO

1 pound fava beans, washed, ends and strings removed, and cut into bite-size pieces
1 medium onion, diced
¼ cup olive oil
salt to taste
1 fresh lemon

1. Bring water to a boil. Add beans and simmer until beans are soft, about 8-10 minutes.
2. While beans cook, sauté onions in olive oil until soft and golden.
3. Drain beans and cool. Place in a serving bowl, add salt and mix.
4. Remove onions from heat and cool for a few minutes before adding to beans. Mix well.
5. Arrange lemon slices decoratively.

▶ *Serves four*

Onion Salad
PIVAZ

2 vidalia onions or 2 white onions thinly sliced lengthwise
1 teaspoon salt
1 tablespoon tomato paste
1 teaspoon pepper paste or cayenne pepper to taste
1 small bunch parsley, minced
1 medium bell pepper, minced

1. Gently knead onions and salt together in a bowl. Add the next three ingredients and mix well.
2. Place onions on a serving plate and spread parsley and peppers over onions.

Note: Great with shish kebab

▸ *Serves six*

Grilled Tomatoes
Khirvoodz Banadoora

Using flat skewers, thread 6-8 medium, firm and ripe tomatoes. Thread whole tomatoes from the stem end. Grill on low charcoal fire until the skins begin to break. Peel tomatoes and arrange them around onion salad.

▸ *Serves six*

Grilled Vegetables

We grill many other vegetables, some threaded through skewers or on heavy aluminum placed over the grilling rack.

Mushrooms: Thread whole steamed mushrooms on skewers.

Asian eggplant: With every fourth piece of shish kebab, add a cubed eggplant.

Peppers and onions: Quartered and grilled on aluminum.

Zucchini: Slice lengthwise and sprinkle with salt and let rest 10-15 minutes. Pat dry and place zucchini over greased aluminum foil. Grill 6-8 minutes on each side.

Note: See Sauces section for the lemon juice and garlic recipe to serve with grilled vegetables.

Grilled Corn on the Cob
Khirvoodz Girig

1. Remove husks and silk from corn.

2. Prepare charcoal fire. After the smoke and flames have subsided, place ears of corn on the grill. Turn frequently to roast evenly.

Roasted Eggplant
Khirvoodz Siv Bedinjoon

1. Preheat oven to 400° F.
2. Using a sharp knife, prick an eggplant at several places. Place it on a tray covered with aluminum foil and roast.
3. Eggplant is done when it's soft inside. Take care not to make it mushy.
4. Remove from oven and place it on a plate. Cut in half lengthwise but not through the bottom skin. Fan out two halves to cool.
5. Carefully scoop out eggplant from skin. This can be done by placing a dinner knife on the skin and scrapping the pulp. Remove excess seeds.

Note: Roasted eggplant keeps in the refrigerator for about five days.

Uses for roasted eggplant:

1. Cut lengthwise and place inside meat pizza (*lahmajoun*) – see recipe.
2. Cut into bite-size pieces and chill. Add yogurt and mint for a cool salad.
3. Use for making baba ganoush.
4. Use to make eggplant and walnut salad – see recipe.

Parsley and Egg Patties
Adjo

    1 large bunch Italian parsley
    1 bunch scallions
    5-6 teaspoons of fresh chopped mint or 3 teaspoons dry mint
    3-4 eggs lightly beaten
    hot pepper flakes to taste
    salt to taste
    1 cup olive oil

1. Wash vegetables, pat dry and cut fine (not quite minced). Add remaining ingredients and stir.
2. Heat olive oil in a large skillet over moderate heat.

3. Drop large serving spoonfuls of mixture gently into the hot oil. Repeat the process until the skillet is filled with patties, about 7-8 spoonfuls.
4. Cook until lightly brown for about 4-5 minutes. Turn and brown other side.
5. Transfer patties to a platter covered with paper towels.
6. Serve warm with salad, sliced tomatoes, or pink pickles.

Note: Use *adjo* to make excellent sandwiches.

▸ *Serves 4*

Baked Eggplant with Tomato and Garlic
IMAM BAIYELDEH

>6 baby eggplants
>¼ cup olive oil
>6-8 cloves garlic, pealed and sliced in half
>3 medium ripe tomatoes, peeled, seeded and chopped
>½ cup water
>salt to taste

1. Preheat oven to 300° F. Wash and stem eggplants. Peel off skin vertically, about half inch apart. Make several 1 inch slits lengthwise into each eggplant. Salt lightly and let drain for half hour. Rinse and pat dry.
2. Heat olive oil in skillet and brown eggplant lightly on all sides. Remove and set aside.
3. Cover pan with aluminum foil. Distribute the garlic slices in eggplant slits and arrange eggplants in the pan.
4. Add chopped tomatoes over eggplants. Sprinkle lightly with salt.
5. Add the water around the eggplant and bake for 45 minutes to 1 hour or until eggplants are soft.

▸ *Serves six. Serve hot or cold with lemon slices.*

Fried Eggplant
DABGOODZ SIV BEDINJOON

>1 large eggplant or 3 small ones
>½ cup olive oil

salt

1. Wash and pat dry eggplant. Remove stem. If large, cut in half or into quarters, then slice into quarter inch thick pieces lengthwise. If small, just slice into quarter inch-thick pieces lengthwise (some of the pieces will be oval-shaped). Sprinkle slices with salt and place in colander to let juices drain for half hour. Pat dry.
2. Heat oil in a large skillet and fry eggplant slices until golden on both sides. Transfer and let drain on plate covered with paper towels.

▸ Serves 4. Serve hot or cold with lemon wedges or tomato relish (see recipe).

Fried Eggplant with Eggs
Havgutoom Dabgoodz Siv Bedinjoon

1 large eggplant or 3 small ones
2-3 eggs
½ cup olive oil
salt
hot pepper or cayenne pepper flakes—optional

1. Follow directions in step 1 for Fried Eggplant above.
2. Beat eggs and pepper together. Dip each eggplant slice in egg mixture and continue with step two for frying and draining.

▸ Serves four. Serve hot or cold with tomato relish (see recipe).

Fried Zucchini
Dabgoodz Tuttom

3 small zucchini
¼ cup olive oil
salt

1. Scrub zucchini under cold water and pat dry
2. Remove stem. Slice into quarter inch pieces lengthwise. Sprinkle slices light-

ly with salt and place in colander to let juices drain for 10 minutes. Pat dry.
3. Heat oil in a large skillet and fry zucchini slices until golden on both sides. Zucchini fries slowly. Transfer and let drain on plate covered with paper towels.

▸ *Serves four. Serve hot or cold with lemon juice with crushed garlic – see sauce recipe.*

BEVERAGES
YOGURTS & CHEESES
BREADS
APPETIZERS
SALADS
SOUPS & STEWS
VEGETABLES

Pilaf

STUFFED VEGETABLES
MEAT DISHES
TOKEN FISH
PICKLES, RELISH & SAUCES
SNACKS
DESSERTS

There are many varieties of pilaf and various ways of making them. Many people are familiar with rice pilaf. In Musa Dagh, the pilaf specialty was made with bulgur and vegetables. The vegetable selection varied according to which were in season – zucchini, eggplant, potatoes, green beans or cabbage.

Rice Pilaf
Urzoom Pilaf

> 3 tablespoons of clarified butter (page 32)
> 1 cup long grain rice
> 2 bundles of vermicelli noodles broken into 1 ½ inch pieces or ⅓ cup angel hair spaghetti cut into one inch pieces
> 3 cups of boiling water or broth, preferably lamb
> salt to taste

1. Melt butter in a saucepan on low heat. Add noodles (or spaghetti) and stir gently until the noodles turn light brown.
2. Add rice and stir for two minutes. Add water or broth, salt, and stir once. Cover and simmer on very low heat.
3. Cook until all the liquid is absorbed, about 20-30 minutes. If rice is not cooked to desired consistency, add tablespoonfuls of hot water accordingly.
4. Remove from heat and let pilaf rest covered for ten minutes.

▸ *Serves four*

Bulgur Pilaf with Chick Peas
Ciciroom Geurgeud Abeur

This is excellent with *gooloogoos*.

> ¼ cup dry chick peas—place in a bowl, cover with cold water and soak overnight
> 3 tablespoons of clarified butter (page 32)
> 2 bundles of vermicelli noodles broken into 1 ½ inch pieces or ⅓ cup angel hair spaghetti cut into one inch pieces
> 1 cup bulgur #3

3 cups of boiling water
1 teaspoon tomato paste
salt to taste

1. Drain chick peas and place in saucepan and cover with water. Simmer until soft.
2. In another saucepan brown noodles (or spaghetti) in butter on low heat. Add bulgur and stir for two minutes.
3. Add water, tomato paste, salt. Drain and add chick peas and stir once. Cover and simmer on very low heat until all the liquid is absorbed, about 20-30 minutes.
4. Remove from heat. Keep covered and let pilaf rest for ten minutes.

▸ *Serves four*

Pilaf with Meat
MEYKHANA PILAF

⅓ pound lean ground meat, preferably lamb
2 tablespoons clarified butter (page 32)
1 medium chopped onion
1 medium green pepper, seeded and chopped
½ teaspoon black pepper
½ teaspoon allspice
salt to taste
cayenne to taste
1 ripe tomato, skinned, seeded and chopped
1 cup bulgur #3
2 cups boiling water

1. In a pot large enough to hold all the ingredients, cook meat on low heat in two tablespoons of cold water. Stir several times.
2. After the water is absorbed, add butter and the next six ingredients up to tomato. Mix well and cook until the vegetables wilt.
3. Add tomato and cook several more minutes.
4. Add bulgur, boiling water, cover and simmer 25-40 minutes until the water

is absorbed.
5. Remove from heat, cover, and let pilaf rest for ten minutes.

▸ *Serves four*

Fava Bean Pilaf
PAGLOOM GEURGEUD ABEUR

    1 pound fresh fava beans, both shell and pods
    2 cups water
    1 cup bulgur #3
    1 ripe medium tomato, skinned, seeded and chopped
    1 teaspoon tomato paste
    salt to taste
    ¼ cup olive oil
    1 medium onion, diced

1. Wash fava beans, remove string, and cut into one inch pieces. If shells are tough, discard and only use pods.
2. Bring water to boil, add beans and cook until slightly soft, about six minutes.
3. Add bulgur, tomato, tomato paste and salt. Stir once. Bring to boil, cover, and simmer about 30 minutes or until water is absorbed.
4. While pilaf is simmering, sauté onion in olive oil until soft and lightly browned.
5. Remove pilaf from heat, add olive oil and onions. Stir once, cover, and let pilaf rest five minutes.

▸ *Serves four*

Potato Bulgur Pilaf
KAMOOM GEURGEUD ABEUR

    2 cups water
    2 medium red potatoes, washed, peeled, and cut into bite-size pieces

1 cup bulgur-# 3
1 medium ripe tomato, skinned, seeded, and chopped
1 teaspoon tomato paste
salt to taste
¼ cup olive oil
1 medium onion, diced

1. Bring water to boil. Add potatoes and cook for five minutes.
2. Add bulgur, tomato, tomato paste and salt. Bring to a boil, cover and simmer about 20 minutes or until water is absorbed.
3. While pilaf is simmering, sauté onion in olive oil until soft and lightly browned.
4. Remove pilaf from heat, add onions and olive oil to pilaf and stir once. Cover and let pilaf rest five minutes.

▸ *Serves four*

Green Bean Bulgur Pilaf
LEYVASOOM GEURGEUD ABEUR

½ pound green beans
2 cups water
1 cup bulgur #3
1 ripe tomato, skinned, seeded and chopped
1 teaspoon tomato paste
salt to taste
¼ cup olive oil
1 medium onion, sliced lengthwise

1. Cut beans into 1 ½ inch pieces.
2. In large saucepan, bring water to boil. Add green beans and cook for five minutes.
3. Add bulgur, tomato, tomato paste and salt.
4. Bring to a boil, cover and simmer about 20 minutes or until water is absorbed.
5. While pilaf is simmering, sauté onions in olive oil until soft and lightly

browned.
6. Remove pilaf from heat, add onions and olive oil to pilaf and stir once. Cover and let pilaf rest five minutes.

▸ *Serves four*

Bean-Potato Bulgur Pilaf
Leyvasoom-Kamoom Geurgeud Abeur

    2 cups water
    ¼ pound green beans cut into 1 ½ inch pieces
    1 medium red potato, peeled and cut into bite-size pieces
    1 cup bulgur #3
    1 ripe tomato, skinned, seeded and chopped
    1 teaspoon tomato paste
    salt to taste
    ¼ cup olive oil
    1 medium onion, sliced lengthwise

1. Bring water to boil in a large saucepan.
2. Add beans and cook for four minutes. Add potatoes and cook for additional four minutes. Add bulgur, tomato, tomato paste and salt. Bring to a boil, cover and simmer about 20 minutes or until water is absorbed.
3. While pilaf is simmering, sauté onions in olive oil until soft and lightly browned.
4. Remove pilaf from heat, add onions and olive oil to pilaf and stir once. Cover and let pilaf rest five minutes.

▸ *Serves four*

Mixed Vegetable Pilaf
Turkhash Geurgeud Abeur

Depending upon personal favorites and fresh vegetables in season, bulgur pilaf can be made with one or more vegetables. In addition to the ones described above, one can also use cabbage, eggplant and zucchini.

For cabbage: ½ small cabbage, remove stem and cut leaves into bite-size pieces.

For eggplant and zucchini: select small ones, and cut into bite- size pieces.

1. First cook vegetables.
2. Use the same amount of ingredients and follow the same procedure for making green bean or potato-bulgur pilaf.

Lentil Pilaf
MUJADDARAH

>   2 cups water
>   1 cup green lentils, rinsed several times in cold water and drained
>   1 cup bulgur #3
>   1 teaspoon tomato paste
>   salt to taste
>   ⅓ cup olive oil
>   4 large onions, halved and thinly sliced lengthwise

1. In a pot large enough to hold all the ingredients, place lentils and one cup of water. Bring to a boil and cook for five minutes.
2. Add the second cup of cold water and bring to boil and cook an additional five minutes.
3. Add bulgur, tomato paste, salt, cover and simmer uncovered until water is absorbed, about 20 minutes.
4. While Mujaddarah is cooking, sauté onions in olive oil until lightly browned.
5. Remove onions from olive oil and put onto a plate. Pour hot olive oil over Mujaddarah. Mix once, cover, and let rest five minutes.
6. Transfer Mujaddarah to a serving platter and arrange onions on top.

▸ *Serves four*

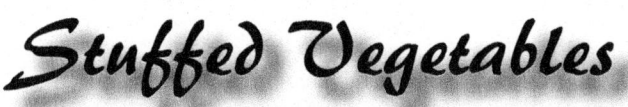

Beverages
Yogurts & Cheeses
Breads
Appetizers
Salads
Soups & Stews
Vegetables
Pilaf

Stuffed Vegetables
Doolmo & Sarmo (Dolma & Sarma)

Meat Dishes
Token Fish
Pickles, Relish & Sauces
Snacks
Desserts

Fillings (Kima)

Doolmo a term used to describe anything stuffed, is a favorite dish in the Middle East. Stuffed grape leaves have become very popular and are now available in cans. Taste in *doolmo* varies according to spices, chosen ingredients, and the method of preparation. Here are three recipes for fillings, one with meat and two meatless. The fillings (both meat and meatless) can be prepared ahead and refrigerated.

We call stuffed leaves, *sarmo* rather than *doolmo*. For us, any leaves wrapped with filling is *sarmo* while stuffed vegetables are *doolmo*. Plain yogurt accompanies our *doolmo* and *sarmo* dishes.

Meat filling

This filling is for grape leaves, cabbage leaves and all vegetables that can be hollowed out.

- ¾ cup long grain white rice
- ½ pound lean ground meat, preferably lamb
- 1 medium ripe tomato, peeled, seeded, and diced
- 1 tablespoon tomato paste
- juice of one lemon
- ½ teaspoon ground allspice
- ½ teaspoon ground black pepper
- cayenne pepper to taste
- salt to taste

1. Combine all the ingredients for the filling. Mix well and set aside.
2. The preparation and cooking for each vegetable varies and is discussed with each one.

Note: Leftover filling can be placed in a small dish, placed over vegetables and cooked in the same saucepan.

▸ *Serves six*

Meatless Rice Filling
Seud 1

This meatless rice filling may be used for stuffing grape leaves and Swiss chard only. Follow preparation steps outlined for individual vegetables.

    1 medium onion, diced
    4 tablespoons olive oil
    2 ripe tomatoes, peeled, seeded and chopped
    1 tablespoon tomato paste
    juice of ½ lemon or adjust to taste
    ½ teaspoon allspice
    cayenne pepper to taste
    1 cup long grain white rice
    ¼ cup chopped walnuts
    salt to taste
    ½ cup chick peas—soak overnight, cook until soft

1. Sauté onions in olive oil until soft and translucent.
2. Add the tomatoes and the remaining ingredients up to the rice.
3. Bring mixture to a boil, add rice and simmer covered until all the juices are absorbed. Stir occasionally.
4. Set filling aside to cool. Add walnuts and chick peas. Mix well.

▸ *Serves six*

Meatless Bulgur Filling
Seud 2

This filling is used for cabbage only.

    1 teaspoon salt
    1 cup bulgur #3
    1 teaspoon allspice
    1 teaspoon tomato paste
    juice of one lemon

cayenne pepper to taste
salt to taste
3 medium onions, diced
3-4 tablespoons olive oil

1. Soak bulgur with ¼ cup of cold water in a bowl for about 15 minutes. Add ingredients from allspice up to onions. Mix well and set aside.
2. Sauté onions in olive oil until translucent. Add to bulgur mixture.

▸ Serves six

The Stuffed Vegetables

Stuffed Grape Leaves
DILLEH DIRIVOOM SARMO

For filling: use either the meat or meatless rice filling found above.

1 jar of preserved grape leaves (found in Middle Eastern markets or gourmet section of some grocery stores) or 50 fresh grape leaves.

1. For preserved leaves: Rinse with cold water and drain well.
2. For fresh grape leaves: Dip in hot water and cook until limp. Immediately place in cold water and drain well.
3. Spread a grape leaf on a flat surface with smooth side down and stem side facing towards you. Place a spoonful of filling near stem end and spread mixture to form a neat cylindrical-sausage shape. Fold both sides over filling and roll grape leaf from stem side to tip. Follow this procedure for remaining grape leaves.
4. Line the bottom of a saucepan with several grape leaves.
5. Arrange stuffed grape leaves seam side down in a saucepan. Cover with several grape leaves and place a small inverted plate on top. Add about two inches of cold water. Bring to a boil., cover and simmer on low heat for about an hour or until rice is soft. Check and add warm water if needed.

▸ Serves six

Stuffed Cabbage Leaves
LUKHANOOM SARMO

Use either the meat or meatless rice filling found above.

    1 medium-size cabbage
    1 ½ teaspoons salt

1. Bring water and a teaspoon of salt to a boil in a large saucepan. Place cabbage in the water with the stem end down. The water should cover two thirds of the cabbage.
2. Simmer a few minutes. Cut cabbage leaves at stem end and separate gently. Remove leaves and place in colander to drain. Continue removing cabbage leaves until you reach the tight center cabbage head. See note.
3. Cut larger leaves in half and remove the hard center stem. Place a spoonful of stuffing along the stem, leaving one inch on both sides. Fold sides over stuffing and roll cabbage leaf. Complete this process for all leaves.
4. Line the bottom of a saucepan with a few cabbage leaves. Arrange the stuffed cabbage leaves seam-side down. Place several leaves over them and add a small inverted plate on top. Add water to cover up to one third of the arranged cabbage leaves rows.
5. Sprinkle ½ teaspoon salt and bring to a boil.
6. Cover and simmer for one hour or until rice is soft.

Note: Cabbage head can be opened, filled and cooked. Or save to use for other recipes.

▸ *Serves six*

Stuffed Eggplant, Zucchini & Yellow Squash
SIV BADINJNOOM, TUTMOOM DOOLMO

Use either the meat or meatless rice filling found above.
    Look for small (6) unblemished eggplants or firm (6) squashes. Larger zucchini may be cut in half.

Vegetable scoop tool

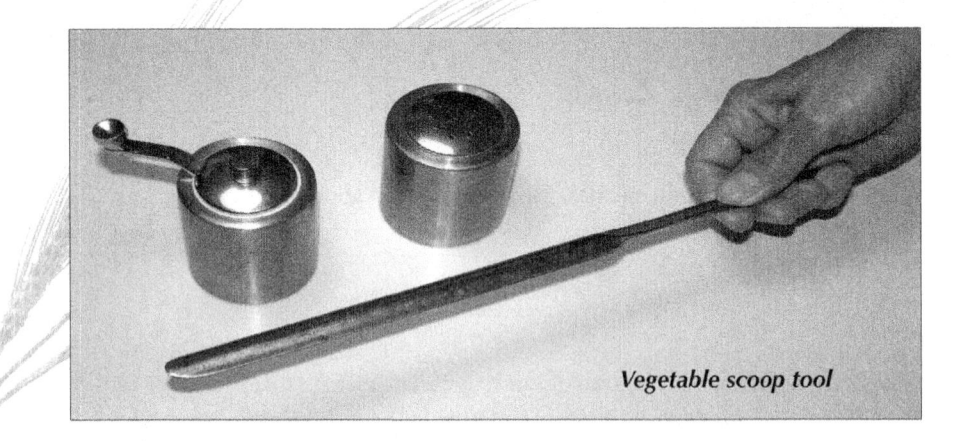

1. Cut off half inch of stem ends of vegetables and save for caps.
2. With a sharp paring knife or a vegetable peeler, carefully scoop* out the pulp to hollow each vegetable to a quarter inch shell. For yellow squash, use the tines of a fork to gently score the skin to create striped pattern (see photo). Rinse vegetables with cold water and drain upside down.
3. Fill each hollowed shell, adding some of the juices accumulated at the bottom of mixture. Stuff each vegetable to half inch of opening and cap with saved stems.
4. Arrange vegetables with stems up in a saucepan. Place an inverted plate inside the pot to cover the vegetables. Add enough water to cover one third of the vegetables.
5. Bring water to boil. Cover and gently simmer for one hour or until vegetables and rice are soft.

*Note: A special narrow scooping tool can be found in Middle Eastern markets.

▸ *Serves six*

Stuffed Peppers
HAMIMOOM DOOLMO

Use either the meat or meatless rice filling found above.

Depending on size, 4 to 6 red or green peppers, as preferred

1. Using a sharp pairing knife, cut a circle around stems.
2. Carefully remove pepper stems, seeds, and inside veins. Rinse peppers with cold water and drain upside down.
3. Follow directions for stuffed eggplant, zucchini and yellow squash (page 91), steps 3-5.

Stuffed peppers and green and yellow squash, cooked and ready to eat

Stuffed Tomatoes
BANADOOROOM DOOLMO

Use either the meat or meatless rice filling found above.

Depending on size, select 5 to 7 firm tomatoes.

1. Using a sharp pairing knife, cut a circle around stems.
2. Carefully remove tomato stems. Remove the tomato pulp and seeds to save

for another use.
3. Follow directions for stuffed eggplant, zucchini and yellow squash (page 91), steps 3-5.

Stuffed Swiss Chard
ZULKHOOM SARMO

Use either the meat or meatless rice filling found above.

One large bunch Swiss chard

1. Dip chard leaves in boiling water for one minute, then immediately place in cold water. Drain well.
2. Large chard leaves may be cut in halves or quarters along the stem if necessary. For filling and cooking, follow directions described in stuffed cabbage leaves.

BEVERAGES
YOGURTS & CHEESES
BREADS
APPETIZERS
SALADS
SOUPS & STEWS
VEGETABLES
PILAF
STUFFED VEGETABLES

Meat Dishes

TOKEN FISH
PICKLES, RELISH & SAUCES
SNACKS
DESSERTS

Baked Vegetables with Meat
Tava

    6 cups cold water
    ½ pound cubed lean meat, preferably lamb
    2 large red potatoes peeled and cut into bite-sized pieces
    1 medium onion, coarsely chopped
    2 medium tomatoes, peeled, seeded and cut into chunks
    1 baby eggplant cut into one inch cubes
    1 small zucchini, scraped and cut into cubes
    1 bell pepper seeded and cut into cubes
    salt to taste
    black pepper, cayenne pepper, and allspice to taste

1. Preheat oven to 500° F. Bring meat and 3 cups of water to a boil in a saucepan. Simmer for several minutes. Drain and wash meat and saucepan. Return meat to saucepan with the remaining 3 cups of water. Bring to a boil and simmer until water has evaporated to about 1 ½ cups.
2. While meat is cooking, cover a shallow baking pan 9x13 with aluminum foil. Add potatoes, onions and tomatoes, mix well, and bake 40 minutes.
3. Add eggplant, squash and cubed peppers. Continue baking, gently stir several times.
4. Add meat and the cooking liquid to the vegetables. Add salt and spices, mix well. Continue baking for additional 20-30 minutes.

▸ *Serves four*

Baked Dumplings
Manti

Filling for dumplings

    1 pound ground lean meat, preferably lamb
    1 medium onion, minced
    salt to taste
    black pepper, cayenne pepper and allspice to taste

½ to 1 cup lamb or beef broth
1 quart plain yogurt for topping

1. Mix the first 4 ingredients together.
2. Place in refrigerator while preparing dough for dumplings.

Dough for dumplings

2 ½ cups all purpose flour
½ teaspoon salt
lukewarm water to form dough

1. In a bowl mix flour and salt. Gradually add water to form into dough. Knead well and divide into four balls.
2. Place balls on a floured tray and cover with cloth. Add plastic sheet over cloth and let dough rest 6-8 hours.
3. Place one ball on a floured surface and sprinkle flour on a rolling pin. Roll dough into a thin sheet, adding additional flour if dough is sticky.
4. Cut dough with a sharp knife into 2 x 1 ½ inch rectangles. Place filling in center and press short ends together tightly. Center should remain open. The *manti* will look like a little boat.
5. Preheat oven to 350° F.
6. Arrange *manti* on a well-greased circular baking pan, starting from the outer edge and working toward the center.
7. Bake until the *manti* is lightly browned.
8. Add broth to cover *manti* evenly and continue baking until the broth is absorbed. The amount of broth depends upon the size of the baking pan.
9. Prepare yogurt by cooking it on low heat, stirring constantly for about 10 minutes. Do not bring to boil.
10. Remove *manti* from oven and pour the yogurt over it.

▸ *Serves four*

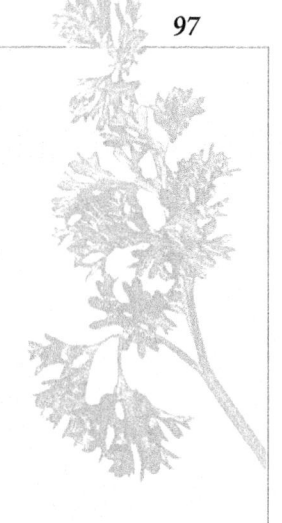

Shish Kebab

Our kebabs are cooked in a rectangular-shaped grill that is 3 to 4 inches deep. We use coals from oak burned in our fireplace which probably burn a bit cooler than commercial briquettes.

1 medium onion, coarsely chopped
1 medium tomato, coarsely chopped
1 tablespoon olive oil
½ cup white wine
salt to taste
1 small leg of lamb, trimmed of fat, and cut into 1 ½ inch cubes

1. Mix all ingredients (except lamb) together in a bowl.
2. Add lamb and mix well.
3. Cover and refrigerate for 24 hours. Stir periodically.
4. Remove meat from refrigerator half hour before grilling.
5. Prepare charcoal fire.
6. Thread meat on skewers and grill kebab about 2 inches from coals. Never grill kebabs over flames or when the coals are still smoking.
7. Rotate skewers and if necessary rotate individual cubes with a paper towel for even cooking. Do not char the meat.

Marinate the kebab for a day. This keeps it moist during grilling.

8. Grilling time is about 15-20 minutes.

Note: Good with grilled tomatoes arranged around onion salad.

▶ *Serves six*

Ground Meat Kebab
LULEH KEBAB

    2 pounds ground lean meat, preferably lamb
    1 small onion, minced
    2 cloves garlic, minced
    1 teaspoon salt
    ½ teaspoon nutmeg
    ½ teaspoon ginger
    ½ teaspoon each of freshly ground allspice and black pepper

1. Knead all the ingredients well. Occasionally moisten hands with cold water and continue to knead until the mixture has a dough-like consistency.
2. Form meat around the center of a flat skewer and shape it into a sausage measuring 6-7 inches long. Smooth the meat with your hand.
3. Continue this process until all the meat is formed onto the skewers.
4. *Grill about 2 inches over charcoal fire after the flames and smoke have died down. Juices may create some smoke.
5. Gently fan the fire and grill kebab about 10 minutes on each side.

Dress luleh kebob with parsley, grilled mushrooms and grilled, peeled tomatoes.

*Note: Ground Meat Kebab may also be baked in a 400° F. preheated oven. Form meat into three inch sausages and place the kebabs on rack. Place pan under the rack to catch the juices. Bake for about 20 minutes, turning kebab several times.

▸ *Serves six*

Kebab with Eggplant
OURFA KEBAB

This is a variation of Ground Meat Kebab. Alternate meat morsels and bite-size pieces of eggplant on skewers. Follow cooking directions for Luleh Kebab.

Liver Kebab
JIGAROOM KEBAB

> 1 lamb liver
> 1 tablespoon olive oil
> 2-3 cloves crushed garlic
> 1 teaspoon ground coriander
> cayenne pepper to taste
> salt to taste

1. Cut liver into bite-size cubes, rinse with cold water and pat dry with paper towels.
2. Place liver cubes into a bowl and add the remaining ingredients and mix well. Cover and refrigerate for one hour.
3. Grill liver kebab following steps outlined in kebab dishes.

▸ *Serves four*

Barbecued Chicken
KHIRVOODS HOOV

> 4-5 pound chicken
> 1 cup dry white wine
> 1 teaspoon each of allspice and black pepper

2 tablespoons melted butter
2-3 cloves crushed garlic

1. Cut chicken into pieces and wash with cold water. Marinate pieces in wine and spices and refrigerate for 2-3 hours.
2. Place chicken and marinade in a large pot and bring to a boil. Cover and simmer until all the liquid is absorbed. Turn pieces to cook evenly.
3. Brush chicken pieces with melted butter and crushed garlic. Place chicken on the grill. If using charcoal fire, be certain that the flames and smoke have subsided completely. Cook about 30 minutes until golden on all sides.
4. Chicken may be roasted in preheated oven 450° F. for 40 minutes turning the pieces once.

▸ *Serves four*

Meat Pizza
LAHMAJOUN

2 packets active dry yeast
2 teaspoons sugar
1 ¼ cups lukewarm water
4 cups flour
1 tablespoon olive oil
pinch of salt

1. Proof yeast: Pour ¼ cup warm water into a tall glass. Add the two teaspoons sugar and stir until it dissolves. Add the yeast, stir gently and place in warm area. The yeast should bubble and foam within 15 minutes. If not, the yeast is not active and shouldn't be used.
2. Combine flour, salt and olive oil in a bowl. Add the yeast mixture and half of the water and mix well. Gradually add the remaining water and knead for 10 minutes until dough is soft. Add more water if necessary.
3. Place dough in a bowl, cover and wrap with a towel. Place bowl in a warm, draft-free area until dough doubles in size.
4. Shape into 18 balls and place them on a tray. Cover with plastic wrap and lay a towel over the tray. Let rest for half hour while preparing filling.

Filling for Lahmajoun
   1 ½ pounds double ground lean lamb
   1 medium onion
   1 large bunch parsley, preferably flat Italian
   1 green pepper
   1 red pepper
   2 medium tomatoes, skinned and seeded
   1 teaspoon hot pepper
   1 tablespoon tomato paste
   2-3 cloves crushed garlic
   pinch of ginger, cinnamon, allspice
   1 teaspoon lemon juice
   salt to taste
   Crisco for greasing trays

Baked lahmajoun

1. Mince vegetables and mix in a bowl with all the remaining ingredients.
2. Grease several trays lightly with Crisco. Sprinkle flour and shake off excess.
3. Preheat oven to 450° F.
4. Form *lahmajoun*: roll a ball of dough into a 5-6 inch circle, about the size of a tortilla, using flour if necessary. Roll out several circles and place them on the prepared trays. Spread about 3-4 tablespoons of filling evenly on each *lahmajoun*, leaving ¼ inch border all around the circle.
5. Bake until bottoms are lightly brown and the filling is cooked well.

Note: Serve with roasted and chilled eggplant strips (see recipe in Vegetables section). Place strips of eggplant along one side of pizza and roll up.

▸ *Serves six*

Musa Dagh Martadella

1 ½ pounds lean lamb, ground twice in food processor
1 teaspoon salt
½ teaspoon ground nutmeg
½ teaspoon ginger
½ cup fine bread crumbs
10 garlic cloves, peeled and halved
1 egg white
1 tablespoon clarified butter (page 32)
½ cup dry white wine
about ½ cup cold water

1. Knead together the first five ingredients and divide into four portions.
2. Flatten each portion like a pancake about 6-7 inches in diameter and ½ inch thick. Place 4-5 garlic pieces across the martadella. Roll the martadella, covering the garlic and patting the sides and ends together. The martadella should be a roll 2-3 inches in diameter.
3. Dip hand in egg white and smooth each roll well.
4. Melt butter in a pan on low heat and sear the rolls thoroughly.
5. Transfer martadella rolls to a saucepan. Add white wine and enough cold water to cover martadella rolls.

6. Bring to a boil and simmer uncovered for 30 minutes on low heat.
7. Remove from liquid, cool and refrigerate. When ready to serve, cut each roll into ⅓ inch thick slices.

Note: Excellent as an appetizer or sandwiches with pita bread.

▸ *Serves six*

Lamb with Skinless Whole Wheat
HEERISEH

    1 ½ pounds lean lamb, all fat removed
    ¾ cup skinless whole wheat
    7 cups water
    salt to taste

1. Bring meat and three cups of water to a boil in a saucepan. Simmer 2-3 minutes. Drain meat and rinse in cold water, discard the liquid, and wash the saucepan.
2. Wash skinless whole wheat several times in cold water and drain.
3. Return meat to saucepan, add skinless whole wheat and four cups of water and salt. Bring to a boil uncovered and simmer several hours until water is absorbed. Do not stir.
4. Both meat and wheat should be soft. If necessary, add ½ cup of hot water and continue cooking until water is absorbed.
5. Remove from heat and stir vigorously with a wooden spoon until meat and wheat turn into a thick mush, about the consistency of cooked oatmeal.

Note: Good with plain yogurt. Also, before the cholesterol buzz, we poured a few spoonfuls of hot clarified butter and a pinch of ground cumin before serving.

▸ *Serves six*

Barbecued Lamb Chops
PERZOLA

    2-3 lamb chops per person

1. Trim fat from lamb chops.
2. Prepare charcoal fire and let smoke and flames subside. Spread coals evenly.
3. Place chops 2 inches above fire and barbecue slowly, turning frequently until chops are done to individual taste.

▸ *Serve immediately*

Eggplant Boats
Karneyaruk

½ pound lean ground meat, preferably lamb
½ cup + 2 tablespoons water
2 tablespoons butter
1 medium onion, diced
6 baby eggplants
3 medium ripe tomatoes
2 bell peppers
2 tablespoons olive oil
salt to taste

1. Prepare filling. Place ground meat and two tablespoons water in a pan and cook over low heat. Stir several times and cook until the water evaporates.
2. Add butter and diced onion and a pinch of salt. Cook on low heat until onions are translucent. Stir occasionally. The filling can be prepared ahead of time.
3. Preheat oven to 400° F. Wash eggplant, remove stems and pat dry. Peel skin vertically, making a striped pattern.
4. Sauté eggplant all around very lightly in olive oil. Remove from heat and carefully lengthwise, ⅔ the way into each eggplant without going through.
5. Widen the cut with fingers and stuff a heaping tablespoon of meat filling inside each eggplant. Arrange stuffed eggplants, slit side up, in a baking pan covered with aluminum foil.
6. Peel, cut the tomatoes in half, seed and arrange half a tomato over each stuffed eggplant.
7. Seed peppers, cut into strips and arrange them over the tomatoes.

8. Gently add the water to the pan. Don't pour water over the vegetables. Sprinkle a little salt over the vegetables and bake for about 45-50 minutes. Most of the water in the pan will evaporate.

Note: This dish goes well with rice.

▶ *Serves six*

Tripe
PEUR

This dish requires several separate steps of preparation: Blanching, making pockets and filling.

> Lamb or beef tripe
> Cold water
> Vinegar

Blanching the tripe:
1. Wash lamb or beef tripe in cold water. Place in a bowl and add several cups of cold water and one cup of vinegar to cover. Refrigerate overnight.
2. Remove tripe from vinegar, wash and place in a pot, cover with water and bring to a boil. Simmer for 10 minutes.
3. Remove tripe from boiling water and transfer to a cutting board. Scrape both sides well with a knife. Wash again with cold water.

Making Pockets:

Cut tripe into rough rectangular pieces. When stuffed and folded, the pockets will be the size of tennis balls. Put tripe aside and prepare filling.

Filling:

> ½ cup long grain rice
> ½ cup lean ground-lamb
> 1 tablespoon tomato paste
> ½ teaspoon ground allspice
> ½ teaspoon ground black pepper

salt to taste

1. Mix all the ingredients in a bowl with your hands. Divide into the same number of portions as the cut pockets.
2. Place one portion over half of each tripe piece, fold over the other half to form a pocket. Close opening on three sides by sewing the ends together with a large needle and thread or pins. Repeat for the remaining tripe pockets.
3. Place tripe pockets in pot, seam sides up. Add water to cover about bottom ⅓ of pockets and bring to a boil. Cover and simmer about 2-3 hours. Add hot water as needed.
4. Test for done by sticking a fork into the pockets. If necessary, add more boiling water around pockets. Tripe pockets are done when both meat and rice are soft.

▸ *Servings vary with size and number of pockets*

Stewed Liver
HUBULOODZ JIGAR

1 lamb liver
2 tablespoons water
1 tablespoon butter
1 medium onion, diced
2 tomatoes, peeled, seeded, and chopped
1 small bunch parsley, patted dry and chopped
hot pepper flakes, optional
salt to taste

1. Cut liver into small pieces, the size of lima beans.
2. Place in a pan with the water and cook on low heat until water is absorbed. Stir occasionally.
3. Add butter and onions. Continue cooking until onions are translucent, stirring occasionally.
4. Add tomatoes and continue cooking until tomato juices are absorbed. Add salt and pepper flakes. Stir well.

5. Add parsley and mix.

▸ *Serves four*

Stuffed Shoulder of Lamb
AHYAGAI

    6 pounds shoulder of lamb
    ½ cup long grain rice
    ½ pound finally chopped lean lamb
    1 tablespoon tomato paste
    ½ teaspoon black pepper
    ½ teaspoon allspice
    2 dozen roasted pine nuts
    2 cups cold water
    salt to taste

1. Cook rice in 1 cup cold water. Bring to a boil and let simmer for 20 minutes or almost cooked. Let cool.
2. Trim excess fat from rack of lamb and cut pocket through one side so it can be opened. Sprinkle lightly with salt, inside and out.
3. Preheat oven to 350° F. In a bowl, mix the chopped meat with the cooked rice, add the pine nuts, the spices, tomato paste and salt, if needed. Mix well.
4. Insert the rice mixture in the pocket and close the opening with skewers or sew with thread and large needle.
5. Place lamb in a roasting pan with fat side up. Add one cup of water around lamb and bake covered for about 2 hours.
6. Uncover, and continue baking for additional ½ hour or until lamb is soft.
7. Remove pan from oven and remove skewers or thread. Spoon out rice. Carve the meat and arrange decoratively either on top or around rice.

Note: Good with yogurt

▸ *Serves four*

Bachelor's Feast or Father's Specialty
BEYKAR MANJASSAH

    4 tablespoons butter
    1 pound cubed or ground lamb
    6-8 medium potatoes, boiled, peeled and cut into bite-size pieces
    6-8 eggs
    salt to taste

1. In a large skillet, cook the lamb in butter. Add the potatoes and mix.
2. Beat the eggs lightly, add salt, and pour over potatoes and meat. Stir until eggs cook.

Note: A cook can be creative with this recipe and use other favorite ingredients and left overs.

▸ *Serves a hungry dozen*

KEUFTEH

Keufteh (sometimes spelled "Kufta") is a dish of great variety and popular in the Middle East. *Kibbeh* or *sinoorgha*, the diamond-shaped pie dish, is probably the best known *keufteh* and frequently served in restaurants and church bazaars. In Musa Dagh, we had several variations of *keufteh*.

Musa Dagh Steak Tartare
CHEE KEUFTEH (MUSSOOM PORTODJ)

This dish, used usually for appetizer (*mezza*), requires special attention. Use only extra-lean and very fresh lamb.

    1 cup bulgur #1
    ½ pound lamb, ground three times
    1 teaspoon ground cumin
    1 tablespoon pepper paste
    salt to taste

1 small bunch parsley, washed patted dry and minced
1 small bunch scallions, washed patted dry and minced
ice cold water.

1. Add enough ice-cold water to thoroughly moisten bulgur and soak for fifteen minutes.
2. Using cold water, wet hands and knead bulgur for ten minutes.
3. Add the meat, cumin, pepper paste and salt. Keeping hands moist with cold water, knead for additional couple of minutes. Continue kneading until the mixture is soft. Always keep hands moist with cold water. Adjust salt to taste.
4. Pinch off a small piece of the mixture the size of a ping-pong ball. Gently squeeze to form an oval shape and arrange it on a platter. Repeat shaping ovals for the entire mixture.
5. Garnish with chopped parsley and scallion.

Note: Cooked filling for diamond-shaped pies (below) may be served with Musa Dagh steak tartare.

▶ Serves Four

Keufteh Common Ingredients

Making Musa Dagh variations of *keufteh* requires several preparations. One is the filling which can be made ahead of time. The second is the bulgur meat mixture. After kneading, this mixture becomes a shell for forming various shapes to hold the meat filling.

With these mixtures, we make diamond shapes pies, hollowed, round or torpedo-shaped meatballs and flat patties.

Keufteh Meat Filling (referred to below as "filling"): This can be prepared ahead of time.

1 pound lean ground lamb
½ cup water
1 tablespoon butter
1 medium onion, diced

1 teaspoon salt
black and cayenne pepper to taste
½ cup finely-chopped walnuts

1. In a large skillet, cook meat and water on low heat, stirring occasionally.
2. When water evaporates, add butter and remaining ingredients. Continue cooking, stirring frequently, until onions are soft. Add walnuts and mix well. Let rest and refrigerate. Bring to room temperature for use.

Keufteh Bulgur-meat Shell Mixture (referred to below as "shell mixture"): *This cannot be made ahead of time. A food processor can be used for kneading bulgur-meat shell mixture.*

2 cups #1 bulgur
1 pound lean leg of lamb – remove all fat and grind meat three times
2 cups cold water and 4-6 ice cubes
1 ½ tablespoons hot pepper paste
1 teaspoon cumin
salt to taste

1. Add enough cold water to thoroughly moisten bulgur and let soak for 15 minutes.
2. Using cold water with ice cubes, wet hands and knead bulgur for 10 minutes.
3. Add ⅔ of the meat, pepper paste, cumin, and salt. Using the iced water to keep your hands moist, knead for another 10 minutes. The bulgur mixture will become soft and pliable.
4. This mixture now becomes the base for several dishes. The remaining ⅓ of the meat will be used in the recipe to keep the bulgur mixture pliable.

Diamond-shaped Pie
Sinoorgha or Sini Keufteh

keufteh meat filling (page 110)
bulgur-meat shell mixture (above)
olive oil

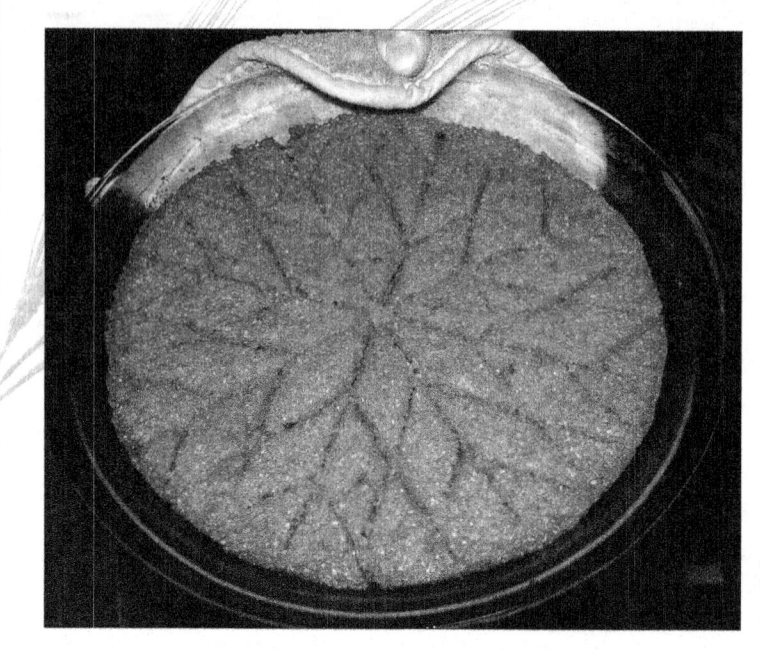

This is the pattern we use for our Sinoorgha. You might want to invent your own.

1. Preheat oven to 350° F. Liberally brush two 9 inch pie plates with olive oil.
2. Divide the **shell mixture** – prepared in steps 1-3 above – into four equal parts. Hands need to be kept moist while preparing. Take one fourth and form it into a patty. Press the patty to cover the bottom of the pie plate evenly, forming a ¼ inch thickness. Repeat to cover the bottom of the second pie plate.
3. Divide the **filling** and spread it evenly on the two pies.
4. Take the remaining ⅓ meat and combine with the two parts of **shell mixture**. Knead while keeping hands moist.
5. Divide this **shell mixture** in half and form two patties. Use each to cover the meat filling of the two pies.
6. Smooth **shell mixture** over the top layer and cut into diamond shapes as shown in photo. Sprinkle one tablespoon of olive oil on top of each pie. Run the tip of a sharp knife around the edge.
7. Bake for about 30 minutes until light brown.

▸ *Makes two pies, Serves 8 to 10*

Stuffed Torpedo-shaped Meatballs
KALOOR SHAMOORGHA

>keufteh meat filling (page 110)
>bulgur-meat shell mixture (page 111)
>olive oil

Iced water is required to form the **shell mixture** into oval-torpedo shapes. If **shell mixture** crumbles while shaping, moisten hands with iced water and knead further. It is more challenging to prepare this dish than the diamond-shaped pie, but worth the effort.

1. Preheat oven to 400° F. Liberally brush a baking pan with olive oil.
2. From the **shell mixture,** take several pieces, each the size of an egg, and set aside. Leave the remaining **shell mixture** uncovered.
3. Keeping hands moist with ice water, cradle one oval piece in your palm. Using the index finger of the other hand, gently poke a hole through one end and press and rotate on the inside. Enlarge the shell to three inches and keep its torpedo shape. The hollowed shell should be thin.
4. Add one tablespoon of **filling** into the opening. Do not stuff the cavity.

Torpedo kaloors and sinoorgha emerge from the oven

5. With moist hands, press and seal the opening into a torpedo shape so that there is space around the **filling** in the shell. Place *kaloor* on oiled baking pan.
6. Repeating steps three and four, continue making *kaloors* using about ⅔ of the **shell mixture**. The remaining **shell mixture** will need additional kneading. Add the remaining ⅓ meat, sprinkle with cold water and knead for 4-5 minutes. Complete making *kaloors* (steps three and four).
7. Gently brush all sides of *kaloors* with olive oil. Bake for about 30 minutes until golden brown.
8. Serve hot with plain yogurt.

Note: Leftover **shell mixture** can be used up by making Top-Tope patties.

▸ *Makes one dozen kaloors*

Top-Tope: 3 Keufteh Variations

Stuffed Bulgur-Meat Patties
Top-Tope 1

Note: You can also use this recipe to finish leftover **filling** and **shell mixture** after making diamond shaped pies or torpedo shaped *kaloors*.

> keufteh meat filling (page 110)
> bulgur-meat shell mixture (page 111)
> olive oil

1. Preheat oven to 400° F. Keeping hands moist, pinch off an egg-size piece of **shell mixture** and roll it into a ball. Flatten it into a circle forming a three inch pancake about ¼ inch thick.
2. Put aside and form another patty.
3. Spread 2 tablespoons of the **filling** on top of one patty. Place the second patty on top of the **filling**. Keep the edges moist and seal the circles together. Continue making patties.
4. Place patties on oiled pans and bake about 20-25 minutes. Turn over until both sides are golden brown.

▸ *Makes one dozen.*

Stuffed Parsley-Walnut Patties
Top-Tope 2

Note: You can also use this recipe to finish leftover **shell mixture** as well as the *kaloor* **fillings** used with dumplings for soups (*kaloor for soups*) – see Soups section.

> bulgur-meat shell mixture (page 111)
> dumpling or *kaloor* filling (page 60)

Follow instructions for Top-Tope 1, steps 1 through 4 substituting the parsley-walnut filling.

▸ *Makes one dozen*

Plain Bulgur Patties
Top-Tope 3

Note: You can also use this recipe to finish leftover **shell mixture**.

1. Preheat oven to 400° F. Pinch off **shell mixture** the size of a ping-pong ball. Keep hands moist and form ¼ inch-thick patties.
2. Bake in oiled (olive) pans for 20-25 minutes until firm.

▸ *Serve hot or cold. Number of patties depends on size and amount of leftover shell mixture*

BEVERAGES
YOGURTS & CHEESES
BREADS
APPETIZERS
SALADS
SOUPS & STEWS
VEGETABLES
PILAF
STUFFED VEGETABLES
MEAT DISHES

Token Fish

PICKLES, RELISH & SAUCES
SNACKS
DESSERTS

Fish du Jour
DZEUG

Here's our one and only fish recipe. Mom had learned the preparation of fish in several ways in Antioch, but in Bitias fish was scarce and not part of our regular diet. Most of the fish Mom served came from our river, Kara Chai, and it was consumed on the day it was caught. We are not sure of the variety-all we know is that they were 6-7 inches long. Today, we eat fish more frequently and, most of the time, follow her favorite procedure regardless of the variety of fish we buy.

> 1 pound fish: sword, whiting, orange roughly, catfish, trout, etc.
> 1 heaping tablespoon pepper paste
> salt, optional
> olive or vegetable oil for frying
> lemon garlic sauce (see recipe in Pickles, Relish & Sauces)

1. Wash fish in cold, running water and pat dry.
2. Spread pepper paste liberally over the fish.
3. Fry in oil.
4. For variation, fish may also be grilled on charcoal fire.

▶ *Serve cold with lemon garlic sauce (see sauces)*

Beverages
Yogurts & Cheeses
Breads
Appetizers
Salads
Soups & Stews
Vegetables
Pilaf
Stuffed Vegetables
Meat Dishes
Token Fish

Pickles, Relish & Sauces

Snacks
Desserts

Green Olives
Badeugh

Olives are one of our favorite foods, for snacks, breakfast and appetizer.

In Bitias, our olives came from our own trees in Chaghlaghan. Pop harvested the green olives when they had matured to their normal size, fat and shiny. Once delivered to Mom, she turned the bitter fruit into a cherished treat. The process, like so many of our foods, was time consuming. Mom crushed each olive with a mallet without damaging the seeds. She then started the process of curing the green fruits with cold water.

> 1 pound green olives
> lots of cold water
> salt to taste

1. With a mallet, crush each olive and let the bitter juices ooze out.
2. Wash the olives in cold water and put them in a jar. Fill the jar with cold water, cover, and place it in a safe corner.
3. After a week, empty the water and replace with fresh cold water. Repeat the process several times. Taste an olive. If still too bitter for your liking, continue process at least one more time. These olives taste different from ones sitting on grocery shelves a long time.
4. In the final stage, dissolve one or more tablespoons of salt in 1 quart of cold water, pour over olives and refrigerate jar.

Note: If you plan to use the olives immediately, the amount of salt may be reduced. In Bitias, since olives were cured and used throughout winter, a large amount of salt was used as a preservative in the final stage.

You can serve *badeugh* plain or combine 3 dozen pitted olives and 1 tablespoon tomato-pepper paste. Mix well.

▸ *Serve with pita chips.*

Ripe Black Olives
ATTON BADEUGH

Black olives, ripened on the tree, are a little shriveled and usually ready for use. They are more oily and not as bitter as green olives.

1. Pit 3 dozen black olives.
2. Add one tablespoon tomato-pepper paste. Sprinkle one teaspoon savory and mix well.

Note: black olives can be purchased at Middle Eastern markets or specialty stores.

▸ Serve with pita chips.

Drained Yogurt with Sautéed Onions
MADZNOOM SEUKH

    1 ½ cups drained yogurt
    3 medium onions, peeled and sliced very thin
    4 tablespoons of olive oil
    1 tablespoon of hot pepper paste—adjust amount according to taste

1. Sauté onions in olive oil on medium heat. Do not brown.
2. Remove from heat immediately and drain excess oil. Let onions cool.
3. In a serving bowl, mix yogurt with pepper paste. Add cooked onions and mix well.

▸ Serve with pita bread

Pepper Paste
EPOODZ HAMIM

For many Musa Daghtsis, red pepper paste is an essential ingredient. Mom usually made several batches, pressed the paste in individual small jars, and sealed the jars with wax. She used the paste throughout the year. In the United States, she prepared the pepper paste and wrapped small portions in plastic wrap. She then put the portions in plastic containers and put them in the freezer.

The pepper paste is used in tabouli, Musa Dagh steak tartare *(chee keufteh)*, onion salad, cheese bread, potato salad and in many other dishes.

Pepper paste can be either hot or mild. The ratio of sweet and hot peppers determines the taste. The following recipe makes mild flavor.

> 5 pounds sweet red peppers
> ½ pound hot red peppers
> 3 teaspoons salt

1. Wash peppers and pat dry. Wearing rubber gloves, cut hot peppers in half and remove the white membranes and seeds. Cut peppers into one inch chunks.
2. Using the steel blade, pulverize peppers in food processor. Add salt and pour peppers into a baking pan.
3. Place the pan over low heat and simmer gently, stirring with a wooden spoon. As the water evaporates, the pepper paste will have the consistency of tomato paste. Paste prepared over a low flame preserves the red color.
4. Place pan aside for a day and stir it once in a while. This will allow additional water to evaporate. The paste should be of thick consistency.
5. Divide into desired portions, wrap in plastic wrap, place in container and freeze.

Note: To make a few of spoonfuls of pepper paste, use five sweet red peppers and one hot pepper. Follow the same procedure and salt to taste.

Pink Pickles
TOORSHO

> 1 small cabbage, about 1 ½ pounds
> ½ dozen small turnips
> ¼ section of a beet or ½ a small beet
> ⅓ cup kosher or coarse salt
> 1 cup apple cider vinegar
> 3 cups water

container for pickles—such as a gallon jar with wide mouth and tight lid

1. Wash all vegetables. Remove tough and wilted leaves and hard core of cabbage. Cut into two inch chunks.
2. Cut turnips into quarter inch pieces.
3. Place vegetables in container and sprinkle ⅔ of the salt. Let rest 2-3 hours.
4. Mix water, vinegar, and stir in remaining salt. Pour over vegetables and make certain that the brine covers them. Add the beet.
5. Cover tightly and set aside at room temperature. Pickles will be ready in 2-3 days.

Summer Pickles
Gananch Toorsho

>18 small and tender string beans
>1 dozen small whole Italian peppers
>½ dozen small green tomatoes, cut crisscross stem end
>½ dozen small pickling cucumbers
>1 cup apple cider vinegar
>3 cups water
>⅓ cup kosher or coarse salt
>1 small hot pepper (optional)
>container for pickles—such as a gallon jar with a wide mouth and tight lid

Follow directions steps 1-5 for pink pickles

Note: Vary the choice and amount of vegetables according to personal preference.

Tomato Relish or Sauce
Jinje

This is a good sauce to use on fried or grilled vegetables or parsley and egg patties (*adjo*).

>2 tablespoons butter

3 medium ripe tomatoes—dipped in hot water, peeled and seeded
1 teaspoon hot pepper flakes or pepper paste
salt to taste
optional: 1 bell pepper diced

1. Melt butter. Cut tomatoes into large chunks and add to butter.
2. Add hot pepper, salt and stir.
3. Bring to a boil and simmer 4-5 minutes.

Note: If using pepper, cook in butter for two minutes before adding tomatoes.

Yogurt-Garlic Sauce
Madznoom Seukhteur

Crush two cloves of garlic. Add one cup of plain yogurt . Serve it cold as a sauce or dip.

Lemon Juice-Garlic Sauce

Mix juice of one or two lemons with two or three cloves of crushed garlic. Sauce goes well with grilled vegetables and fried zucchini.

Canned Grape Leaves
Dilleh Diriv

Stuffed grape leaves now come in cans. Prepared leaves are sold in jars and ready for use. This recipe is for fresh grape leaves.

75 tender, small grape leaves
1 quart water
2 tablespoons vinegar

1. Stack 25 leaves in three separate stacks, shiny sides down with stems in one direction.
2. Bring water and vinegar to a boil. With tongs, pick up each pile by the

stems and dip in the boiling water for 2-3 minutes, until the color changes on both sides of the grape leaves.

3. Remove pile and place shiny side down, end stem end toward you.
4. Starting from the stems, roll up grape leaves to form a cylinder. Tie it with a string.
5. Repeat and place 3 bundles in quart jar. Cover with the same boiling water, seal and store.

Note: When ready to use, rinse a bundle in cold water and squeeze out the water.

BEVERAGES
YOGURTS & CHEESES
BREADS
APPETIZERS
SALADS
SOUPS & STEWS
VEGETABLES
PILAF
STUFFED VEGETABLES
MEAT DISHES
TOKEN FISH
PICKLES, RELISH & SAUCES

Snacks

DESSERTS

Our snacks came from our orchards and fields and most were seasonal: fresh fruit in season and dry fruit in winter. Some of our favorite fruits were plum, apricot, loquat, figs, pomegranate, persimmon and purple mulberry.

Besides the above fruits, we enjoyed a variety of berries, such as wheat berries, myrtle berries and the seeds of pumpkins, water melons and cantaloupes. Although the wheat berries and seeds are edible when fresh, usually they were cleaned, salted and roasted before serving. The list of snacks cannot be complete without adding peas, green fava beans, and chick peas, fresh or dry.

Roasted Seeds
BUZZIR

Preparing seeds: pumpkin, watermelon and cantaloupe

1. Place seeds in a strainer and wash thoroughly under running water removing all fibers.
2. Drain, sprinkle with salt and spread on a tray. Cover with a cheesecloth and dry in the sun.

Roasted seeds

1. Preheat oven to 300° F. Spread cleaned seeds on a tray and roast for a half hour or roasted to your preference. Stir occasionally to roast evenly.
2. Cool and store in jars.

Note: The entire pumpkin seed with shell can be eaten, but we have never done so. We gently crack the tip of the shell between our teeth to create an opening and then extract the seed. This is an acquired skill. Louisa's husband has tried to develop it, contorting teeth, tongue and lips while Louisa has watched in mild hysteria.

Roasted Chick Peas
CICEER EGHAH

Use fresh chick peas. The outer hull is somewhat salty and can be removed before serving. Fresh chick peas can be roasted with or without the hull and with or without a little salt. If roasted with the hull, salt is not added.

1. Preheat oven to 300° F. Spread 1 cup fresh chick peas with hulls on a tray and roast for 30 minutes or to desired firmness. Add salt to taste.
2. Cool and store in jars

Roasted Dry Chick Peas
Khandzoodz Cheur Ciceer

    1 cup dry chick peas
    salt

1. Soak chick peas in cold water overnight.
2. Pick over, rinse, drain well and place in a bowl.
3. Sprinkle with a little salt and mix well.
4. Preheat oven to 250° F. Spread chick peas evenly on a cookie sheet. Roast for 20 minutes. The peas will be dry and soft.
5. Cool and store in a jar

Note: chick peas are a tasty, healthy snack, and excellent in salads.

Fresh Wheat Berries
Tseerin Eghah

Fresh wheat berries cannot be eaten without removing the hulls first, and the easiest way of accomplishing that is to roast them.

    A bunch of fresh berries with long stems

1. Tie the bunch together into a tight bouquet.
2. Prepare a low fire on a charcoal grill and gradually roast the berries by rotating the stems. Once the outer hull begins to burn away, the berries will become loose.
3. Transfer to a bowl, throw away stems, and shake the remaining hulls by tossing them gently for a few minutes.
4. Remove the hulls.

The roasted berries are ready to eat.

BEVERAGES
YOGURTS & CHEESES
BREADS
APPETIZERS
SALADS
SOUPS & STEWS
VEGETABLES
PILAF
STUFFED VEGETABLES
MEAT DISHES
TOKEN FISH
PICKLES, RELISH & SAUCES
SNACKS

Desserts

Sugar Water Syrup

Sugar water syrup is used in several dessert recipes. The syrup is used to sweeten desserts without making them soggy and dense. The difference between the thin and thick syrups given here is their consistency, determined entirely by the time spent in cooking.

> 1 cup water
> 1 cup sugar
> thin slice of lemon

Thin syrup for zeungool (page 136) and keunafo (page 131):

Place the ingredients in a small pot and bring to a boil. Simmer on low heat for half and hour and stir a couple of times.

Thick syrup for baklava and other phyllo desserts (page 139):

Place the ingredients in a small pot and bring to a boil. Simmer on low heat for 45 minutes to an hour and stir a couple of times

Rice Pudding
ZERDA

> ¼ cup long grain white rice
> 1 quart milk
> ¼ cup sugar
> ground cinnamon

1. Add ¼ cup long grain white rice to 1 quart of milk and bring to boil.
2. Simmer for about one hour. Stir pudding occasionally, scraping milk from sides of saucepan.
3. Add ¼ cup sugar. Stir and taste to adjust sweetness. Let simmer 2-3 additional minutes.
4. Pour into individual serving dishes.
5. Serve warm or cold sprinkled with cinnamon.

▸ *Serves six*

Young Walnut Preserve
OUNGHAZEH ANOUSH

Walnuts are classified "young" when the inner core is soft like Jell-o and the outer shell is green, not wooden. At young stage, the fruit is bitter and its juices stain hands and clothes. Some nuts, such as almonds, are edible at their green stage, but not walnuts.

The directions we have for young walnut preserve comes from our friend Odette Babikian. It was her mother's original recipe for 100 walnuts and written in Armeno-Turkish. She translated it for us and we reduced the recipe to 24 nuts and adjusted the ingredients accordingly.

Preparing the nuts

    2 dozen young walnuts
    pinch of salt
    cold water

1. Wearing plastic gloves, use a thin sharp knife to peel the glossy outer layer of the nuts and remove the stem tip. Place in a bowl, cover with cold water, add salt and stir. Place in a safe corner. Do not disturb.
2. After a week, change the water and continue changing a couple of times a day for several weeks or until the nuts lose their bitter taste. At this stage the nuts may be partially "cured."
3. Bring a pot of water to a boil, add the walnuts and let boil for about two minutes. Drain nuts, rinse under running water and return to bowl. Cover with water and return to room temperature.
4. With a sharp knife make a crisscross pattern at the blossom end of each nut. Return nuts to a bowl and cover with cold water again. Change water several times a day for a couple of days.

Prepare syrup and combine with nuts

    3 cups sugar
    2 ½ cups water
    sliver of fresh lemon
    a dozen cloves

1. Bring sugar, water and lemon to a boil. Lower heat and let simmer for several minutes. Remove from heat and let syrup cool completely.
2. Pat the nuts dry and transfer to a clean bowl. Pour syrup over nuts and let stand for 24 hours.
3. Remove nuts from syrup and bring syrup to a boil. Add the cloves and simmer until syrup thickens. Cool thoroughly.
4. Place nuts in a jar, add the cold syrup, cover and refrigerate.

Note: Young walnut preserve is usually served with demitasse coffee for guests on special occasions.

Shredded Pastry with Walnuts

KEUNAFO I

1 cup sugar
1 ½ cups water
⅛ inch slice of lemon
1 ½ teaspoons ground cinnamon
1 ½ cups finely chopped walnuts
1 pound shredded pastry* (*keunafo*)
¾ cup clarified melted butter (page 32)
1 ½ teaspoon ground cinnamon

1. Bring water, sugar and lemon slice to a boil. Simmer for about 12 minutes. Set aside to cool.
2. Mix cinnamon and walnuts. Set aside.
3. In a double boiler steam the pastry. Cover the top with a towel until the pastry is soft. Preheat oven to 400° F.
4. Remove pastry, place in a pan and pour the butter over it. Mix well until the pastry is completely covered with butter.
5. Divide pastry in half and spread one portion into a 9 x 13 baking pan. Pat down evenly.
6. Spread cinnamon-walnut mixture evenly over layer. Add and spread second portion to cover the walnut mixture. Pat down.
7. With a sharp knife, cut pastry into two inch squares and bake until golden brown.

8. Remove from oven and immediately pour lukewarm sugar mixture evenly over the *keunafo*. Cover with a paper towel and a kitchen towel. Let rest for one hour and serve at room temperature.
9. Serve with small pitcher of sugar syrup (page 129) for people to add according to taste.

*Note: Shredded pastry is available in Middle Eastern markets.

▸ *Serves one dozen*

Serve keunafo with a pitcher of sugar syrup on the table.

Shredded Pastry With Cheese
KEUNAFO 2

Substitute curd cheese or Anna's Cottage Cheese for walnut-cinnamon mixture. Follow directions for shredded pastry with walnuts (*keunafo 1*).

Boiled Wheat Berries
HADAG

> ½ cup chick peas soaked overnight
> 1 cup wheat berries
> 5 cups water
> 1 cup coarsely chopped walnuts
> 2-3 tablespoons finely ground anise seeds
> seeds of 2 pomegranates (optional)
> sugar

1. Rinse soaked chick peas and wheat berries in cold water. Place in a saucepan, add the water and bring the two ingredients to a boil.
2. Simmer uncovered on low heat until mixture is soft and the water is absorbed. If necessary, add tablespoons of boiling water and continue cooking. Up to step two can be done ahead.
3. Empty mixture on a serving platter, forming a dome.
4. Sprinkle a little chopped walnuts and pomegranate seeds on the wheat berries.
5. In individual bowls place sugar, anise and the remaining walnuts and pomegranate seeds. Arrange the bowls decoratively for guests to use as *hadag* condiments.

▶ *Serves four to six*

Molasses or Honey Dessert with Bulgur
URBOOM TURKHANO

> 1 cup bulgur #4
> 3 cups water

½ cup molasses or honey or a combination*
chopped walnuts

1. Cook bulgur and water together uncovered on low heat until water is absorbed.
2. Stir in molasses (or honey or combination) and simmer for a few minutes.
3. Pour into pie dish while hot. Let stand about 15 minutes. Refrigerate.
4. Sprinkle with walnuts before serving.

*Note: Use of molasses or honey depends on personal preference and the amount used affects the sweetness of the dessert.

▸ Serves six

Milk Yogurt Dessert
Tdool

1 quart milk, preferably whole
1 cup plain yogurt
sugar to taste
chopped walnuts to taste

1. Bring milk to a boil about 180° F.
2. Remove from heat and immediately add yogurt. Stir and let solids that form settle at the bottom of the pot.
3. When cool, pour mixture into a colander covered with a paper towel.
4. Drain until the mixture is the consistency of cottage cheese.
5. Transfer to a bowl and refrigerate.
6. Before serving, add sugar to taste. Sprinkle with walnuts.

▸ Serves six.

Butter Cookies
Ghoorebia

1 cup clarified butter (page 32)
1 cup sugar

2 ¼ cups all purpose flour

1. Beat the butter and sugar until the mixture is creamy.
2. Add the flour gradually and mix thoroughly. Continue mixing with your hands until dough is soft.
3. With your hands, roll a small ball of dough into two inch length and ¼ inch thickness.
4. Bring the ends together and form a circular cookie about 1 ½ inches in diameter. Press a blanched pistachio or a blanched peanut half at connecting ends.
5. Place cookies on ungreased baking sheets about an inch apart. Bake at 200° F. for about one hour. Do not brown.
6. Remove from oven and cool thoroughly. Cookies will be fragile. Use a knife or a spatula while removing cookies.

▸ *Makes two dozen*

Fruit Juice Pudding
BASSTUK

1 heaping tablespoon cornstarch
1 cup grape juice or apricot nectar
½ cup ground or chopped walnuts
sugar–optional

1. Place cornstarch in a cup. Add a few spoons of juice and stir until smooth.
2. Heat the remaining juice over medium heat. Gradually add the cornstarch mixture, stirring constantly until puddings comes to a boil and begins to thicken. Adjust for sugar.
3. Simmer a few minutes. Remove from heat immediately and pour into small serving bowls.
4. Serve pudding hot or chilled. Sprinkle the walnuts before serving.

▸ *Serves four*

Farina Pudding
CIMIT

> 5 tablespoons clarified butter (page 32)
> ¾ cup farina or cream of wheat
> ½ cup sugar, may use more for sweeter pudding
> 2 ½ cups hot water
> ground cinnamon

1. Melt butter in a pan, add farina and roast, stirring constantly until lightly brown.
2. Transfer pan to sink*. Add hot water gradually while stirring.
3. Return pan to low heat and add sugar. Mix well until sugar dissolves about 2-3 minutes. Sprinkle with cinnamon.

*Note: Pan should be placed in sink because splatter usually occurs when adding water.

▸ Serves six

Farina Pudding with Cheese

For a richer tasting farina pudding, add one cup shredded mozzarella cheese after adding the sugar. Stir well over low heat until cheese melts and blends with the farina.

Fried Dumplings with Syrup
ZEUNGOOL

> ½ packet active dry yeast
> ¼ cup water for proofing yeast
> 1 teaspoon sugar
> 1 ½ cups flour
> ¾ to 1 cup water
> canola or olive oil for frying and oil in a bowl for dipping teaspoon

1. Proof yeast: Pour ¼ cup warm water into a tall glass. Add the two tea-

spoons sugar and stir until it dissolves. Add the yeast, stir gently and place in warm area. The yeast should bubble and foam within 15 minutes. If not, the yeast is not active and shouldn't be used.
2. Add yeast to the flour and mix.
3. Add water and mix well. The dough should be soft (like pancake batter).
4. Cover and place it in a warm spot and let it rise.
5. Heat oil in a small skillet about two inches deep.
6. Coat a teaspoon with oil. Take a small handful of dough, make a fist and squeeze it through the top of your hand. Scoop a teaspoon of the dough and place it in the hot oil. It will form into a ball. Continue spooning and adding the dough to the skillet. Turn them evenly as they become light brown.
7. Remove the dumplings to drain on paper towels. Continue spooning and frying the dough until it is finished.

Squeeze a ball of dough out of your fist, scoop it up with a teaspoon and drop it in the oil

8. Serve warm or at room temperature with sugar-water, so each person can sweeten them to their taste.

Note: Leftover dumplings can be refrigerated and heated in a low oven before serving.

▸ *Serves six*

Fry dumplings until golden brown then place on paper towel to drain.

Baklava

Baklava

    1 cup water
    1 cup sugar
    ⅛ slice of lemon
    ½ cup finely chopped walnuts
    1 cup clarified melted butter (page 32)
    1 pound phyllo dough

1. Bring water, sugar and lemon to a boil on low heat for 15 minutes or until syrup is slightly thick.
2. Brush 9 x 13 baking pan with clarified melted butter.
3. Remove phyllo dough and with a sharp knife cut the width side in half. Place halves on top of each other. Keep the dough covered with a lightly dampened towel.
4. Layer the phyllo dough in the baking pan and brush every other sheet with melted butter.
5. When about ⅔ of the dough has been layered, spread walnuts evenly. Finish layering the phyllo and brush the last layer with butter.
6. With a sharp knife, cut pastry into diamond-shaped pieces.
7. Bake in preheated 400° F. for 2-3 minutes. Reduce heat to 350° F. and bake for additional 4-5 minutes. Again reduce heat to 200° F. and bake for 45-50 minutes until golden.
8. Let baklava cool for 15 minutes.
9. For best results, add syrup to baklava when both are lukewarm. We put syrup on sparingly, just spooning it on with a tablespoon. Serve at room temperature.

▸ *Makes about 20 pieces*

Phyllo Rolls
BOORMO

Instead of preparing traditionally sliced baklava the dough can be reshaped into rolls, bird's nests, rosettes and coils.

Make each phyllo roll with a single sheet of dough

Sprinkle walnuts or pistachios across the long edge of the buttered sheet

Fold short edges over, about half an inch

Use the dowel to roll the phyllo to the end

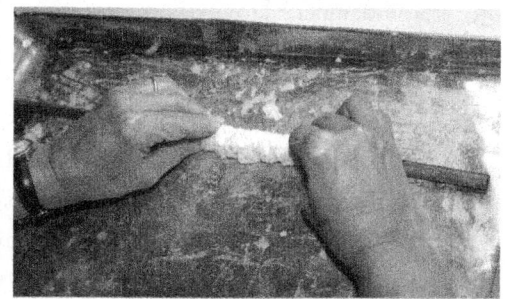

Squeeze ends together, pleating it, until about 4" long (it will gradually expand)

Place on buttered pan and lightly butter each roll

Coil the pastries, end-to-end, in a buttered pie tin and bake

1. Use ingredients for baklava and follow recipe, steps 1-3.
2. Phyllo rolls are formed by rolling individual phyllo sheets. On a flat surface, place a single phyllo sheet.
3. Brush with melted clarified butter and sprinkle one tablespoon walnuts evenly across the long end of one sheet of phyllo, leaving about one inch at each end. Fold each end towards center.
4. Place a thin dowel about ⅓ inch in diameter on the sheet. Fold phyllo over dowel and roll to the end.
5. With fingers at both ends of the dowel, gently squeeze the phyllo sheet to the center, creating a pleated pastry.
6. Carefully push pastry off one end of dowel and place it seam-side down on a buttered baking sheet. Continue with the remaining phyllo sheets.
7. Brush the rolls with melted butter and bake at 350° F. preheated oven for about 25-30 minutes until golden brown.
8. Spoon syrup on each roll when both rolls and syrup are lukewarm. Serve at room temperature.

Note: Rolls may be cut into halves or thirds after removing from oven.

▸ *Makes three dozen rolls*

Bird's Nest or Rosette Baklava

1. Use ingredients* for baklava and follow phyllo roll recipe, steps 1-4. Do not roll phyllo sheet to the end. Leave half inch of sheet at the end.
2. Form the pleated pastry (step 5 above) and push off the dowel. Join the two ends to form a pleated circle and flatten unrolled pastry end to form a base for the rosette.
3. Brush with melted butter and bake at 350° F. in a preheated oven for about 25-30 minutes or until golden brown.
4. Let cool and fill rosette center with coarsely chopped walnuts or pistachios. Add syrup to each rosette.

*Note: We usually use pistachio nuts for rosettes.

Coiled Baklava

1. Use ingredients for baklava and follow phyllo rolls recipe, steps 1-6. Instead of placing rolls on baking sheet, use a buttered pie plate to arrange them in a circle.
2. Start in the center of the pie plate and form a tight circle with a phyllo roll. Continue enlarging the circle by adding pleated rolls. The finished baklava will look like one big pleated coil in the pie plate.
3. Bake baklava following directions for phyllo rolls, steps 7 and 8.

Note: Sprinkle coil with finely chopped pistachio nuts and spoon just a little syrup over the baklava.

After baking, spoon sugar water on the coiled baklava. Be sparing. The most common problem with commercial baklava is its syrupy saturation that ruins flakey layers.

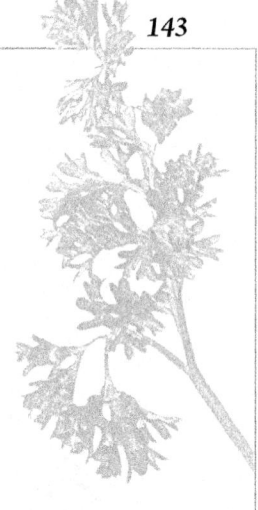

Epilogue

Bitias' main street looking west toward the mosque with part of Musa Dagh is in the background. The mosque had been our church where we attended school. At right is the stone wall that bounds our original house and pushes farther into the street than it had in our day. Of course, there were no electric lines in our time either.

Photo: Richard Furno

Epilogue
by Alberta Magzanian

When we left Musa Dagh in 1939, Anna was nine and I was thirteen. We both have vivid memories of our village of the 1930's. Today, Bitias is called Batiayaz. For some incomprehensible reason, it's called "Tekkepinar" on maps, but as you drive up the road to the village the sign reads "Batiayaz". My sister, Louisa and I learned that when we journeyed there in the summer of 2007. She had never seen Bitias and I promised to give her an extensive tour when we got there. She found it far more beautiful than the pictures she had carried in her mind for six decades.

Before 1939, the population of Bitias, like the other Musa Dagh villages, had been one hundred percent Armenian and had spoken the distinct Armenian dialect, Kistinik. The only Armenian village left on the mountain is Vakef and the residents keep the dialect alive.

Of the Armenian villages on the mountain, Bitias was fairly new, about 300 years old. Settlers from a neighboring village, Haji Habibli, established it and gradually others moved in from areas such as Istanbul, Greece, Antioch, Urfa and Hadjin. By 1939, there were about 220 homes in Bitias scattered on Musa Dagh's foothills.

The whole village was one big orchard. The limestone houses with tile roofs were surrounded by grape arbors and fruit and nut trees. From February through November one could see flowers and fruit everywhere, most commonly apricots, apples, peaches, plums, grapes, oranges, pomegranates, loquats, walnuts, olives, mulberries, and multiple varieties of figs. Most mulberry orchards were outside the village. Their leaves were used to feed silk worms, as silk was one of the important cash industries in the village.

A popular summer resort, Bitias attracted visitors from Aleppo and as far away as Palestine and Egypt. During summer months, the population of the village tripled and, on some weekends, even quadrupled. People came for the scenery, the clean air, the clear, cold spring waters, the fresh fruit and the friendly atmosphere. Our views across the wide valley were spectacular. The valley's eastern border was open and extended about 12 miles by road toward Antioch. To the southeast and far on the horizon sat Jebel Akrah, a volcanic peak that was snow-capped in the winter. All around us, the foothills of Musa Dagh protected the village.

Four major springs irrigated the fields and terraced gardens. The waters sustained the gardens of all the families as well as the influx of vacationers during the summer months. The sound of gushing water could be heard everywhere.

Each spring bore a name in Kristinik. One was named after William John Baker, a British diplomat who had built a house near the spring and had retired there in 1840's. Everyone knew it as "Frankan Aghpayre" translated as "Franks Spring." Why Frank? The villagers, and virtually everyone in the region, called all Europeans, "Franks." Another was called "Kara Poonar," or Black Spring, which roared from the depths of a dark cave and powered two flour mills a half mile south.

Today, there are no Armenians in Bitias. Otherwise, the Bitias I saw in 2007 is much less changed than I imagined. In fact, the house we had lived in is still there.

Life in Bitias

Pop had been in America during World War I and returned to Musa Dagh in 1924 where he met and married Mom. I was born in December of 1925, Anna in July, 1929. Much of our formative youth was lived in Bitias. When we left in 1939, I was 13 and Anne was 10.

Having heard about Bitias all her life, Louisa wanted to know everything during our short, afternoon visit: where had each of the events occurred that she had heard about so often? where had various people lived? and so much more. In many ways, this is an epilogue for Louisa and her family. For her and for anyone else, why would our life be of interest? In part, because Musa Dagh was an "old country", an Armenian homeland that had endured for centuries but is now gone. But more importantly, as children our life style was more of the 19th than the 20th century; we had little electricity, our night light came from kerosene lanterns; our village was virtually self-sustaining for food, industry, repairs, clothing and entertainment. If our family didn't take a direct role in one part of the economy that sustained us, we knew someone who filled another. There are few such places today. This is the short-story of such a self-contained community.

Chaghlaghan

Chaghlaghan was bought by our ancestor around 1800. It extended from the lower elevation woodland of Musa Dagh down through multi-level terraced gardens and stopped at the gorge of Kara Chai a tributary of the Orontes River. The ice-cold streams of Chaghlaghan originated from snow capped peaks to the north. With the melting snow, the water swelled and drowned out any conversation along its banks.

Pop often reminisced about the early days of Chaghlaghan, known throughout Musa Dagh as the Magzanian orchard. He had many visitors there. It became a popular stop for those traveling to work or to Antioch, offering a feast of garden fresh fruit and village gossip.

Pop knew the entire history of the family beginning with the arrival of Movses Chumboudian in Bitias in 1800. In its early days, the Magzanians almost lost Chaghlaghan. Movses Chumboudian's son, Hovagim, took the name Magzanian. He died young leaving behind his young widow, Sima Kadeian Magzanian to take care of the property. Pop, born in 1888, was Sima's grandson. Some village elders tried to swindle her and deprive the children of their inheritance. Although illiterate, Sima went to Antioch to defend her case before the Ottoman courts. She won! The story became well known in Musa Dagh.

Unlike her husband, Sima lived a long, full life, seeing the birth of some of her great grandchildren. At age 98, in 1915, she, along with other Armenians of Musa Dagh, was climbing the mountain to escape the oncoming Ottoman army. She had taken refuge in a cave with her brother and sister-in-law. There, she was found and killed. We often recall the life of our great-great-grandmother and the many years she lived and tended her gardens in Chaghlaghan.

For Pop, Chaghlaghan was the Garden of Eden especially after returning from the United States where he had spent fourteen years working in factories, before and during World War I. When he returned in 1924, Chaghlaghan was divided among the Magzanian descendants. His lots were scattered through a number of orchards and woodlands.

He spent six days a week there from sunrise to sunset, planting, grafting, pruning, bee-keeping and harvesting. Everything alive, vegetation and wildlife, was part of his extended family; he loved it all. The land sustained us and Pop knew all its yields but also its needs and requirements.

He spent time with us explaining how grafting could make fruit trees resistant to disease and increase their yields. After a full day in Chaghlaghan, he would return home laden with fruits and vegetables. Anna and I would wait for him because he always brought us a surprise, whether the season's first ripe peach, a small bouquet of

Looking eastward from Bitias across the Orontes River valley. The hills have been logged yielding this view of ordered rows and dots of newly planted trees.

Photo: Alex Furno

wild violets or an interesting rock. We prized each item. His deep attachment to the land was not unusual at the time. The families of Bitias were sustained by the land.

For Mom, Chaghlaghan was an ideal place for entertaining relatives and friends, usually a picnic along the stream banks. While the children climbed rocks and trees and explored the mountain, the adults prepared a great feast. Parents warned us not to jump in the icy water. They must have known that away from their watchful eyes, we held endurance contests. The one who kept his or her hand immersed in the freezing stream the longest was hero for the day. After our games and ordeals, we would sit down to refreshing melons chilled in the icy waters.

In the entire Chaghlaghan orchard, there was a single rose shrub. Grandfather Hagop Magzanian had planted it decades earlier in the center of the orchard and, when we visited Pop in that section, we would stop and admire it. Long after we left Bitias and, as recently as 1965, we heard that grandpa's rose shrub continued to thrive.

To Anna and me, Chaghlaghan held many mysteries. Somehow it provided us with our food, but it also contained other distinctive treasures. Every spring we gathered crimson poppies under an area of olive trees. In all our wanderings around Musa Dagh, we never found them anywhere else. And Mom could amaze us by taking the petals from Grandfather Hagop's rose blossoms, extract oil, and then sprinkle some on our favorite pudding. To us, it was magic!

We loved visiting Pop in Chaghlaghan. Regardless of how tired or occupied he might be, he made the time to answer our questions. "Where did the waters of the Kara Chai come from?" Pop would explain, pointing to the distant sky in the north where we could barely see the pink hue of Kizil Dagh (Red Mountain).

"What are the names of all those peaks?" "What was life like in America?" When we saw the young men of the village go up the Red Mountain to hunt wild boar, we asked him, "what were they going to do?" He would answer all our questions, whether they were good ones or silly.

During the winter wild boar season, we saw the young hunters returning to the village carrying their prey. The carcasses were suspended from poles that would swing to and fro. We would follow the procession for a block or two treating the hunters as if they were world heroes.

Most of all, we were in awe of Kara Chai below Chaghlaghan. Above the gorge, we could not see descending water, but we were aware of its powerful and angry thunder. Below, we saw its powerful falls and its current. Everything was swept from its path. To us, its roar sounded impatient. Pop had explained that it was headed toward the sea. We thought it had traveled a great distance to reach us and still, impatiently, had such a long, long way to complete its journey. We respected the river and often stopped and strained to listen to its humming, roaring message.

We miss the roar of the springs, the walled terraces and the vegetables and flowers we so often helped Pop gather. Although we lost Chaghlaghan nearly seventy years ago, Anna and I still talk about it as we knew it as children in the 1930's., recalling memories and comparing places where we'd travel to our home in Bitias. In China, we saw so many terraced gardens and in Peru the steep stone steps of Machu Pichu connecting one terraced level with another—these all tug at our memories. To us they felt like home.

On our 2007 trip, we found that the name "Chaghlaghan" still endures. Just beneath the major spring of the garden, we found "Caglayan Cafe"! The spring had been captured and was being used by the cafe for its several fountains and pools. The terraces our great grandfather had built were still there but only a few were being used to grow fruit and vegetables. The rest had gone wild.

Education

In our village, we had two main churches, the Armenian Apostolic Church and a smaller, Armenian Evangelical Church. Each church operated a separate elementary school.

At the Evangelical Church, Anna and I learned Armenian, Arabic and English. Our cousins at the Apostolic school learned French instead of English. Our education also included math, some geography and Armenian history. We loved studying the history of the Armenian nation contained in two skinny primers, going back over two thousand years. The story of our 5th century hero, Vartan the Great, brought us to tears as we learned of his defeat by Persian forces.

Every student had a piece of slate that measured about eight by five inches with two strings running through its wooden frame. One dangling string held a piece of chalk, the other a small damp cloth. When the cloth was dry, a little spit helped clean the slate. All school work–penmanship, math, homework–was performed on that bit of rock.

For homework we memorized Bible verses, poems, vocabulary, and the multiplication table. Most of these tasks we completed at school, leaving our evenings free. In a two-room school house, younger students quickly learned the material covered by the older ones. Anna had memorized my two primers before she entered school. She sat and 'read' the pages, turning them at the correct places, a toddler phenomenon familiar to parents everywhere.

What we lacked in school, we more than made up for in street smarts. The entire village was our school and laboratory. We learned as we roamed, freely testing, tasting and watching; animal feeding, furniture building, mending of clothing and

The Recipes of Musa Dagh

broken tools and even story telling. In the process, we learned a lot about courteous behavior. By early teens, young people had mastered basic village skills as well as some family specialties; care for livestock, planting and harvesting vegetables, pruning trees, helping with the silk industry, knitting sweaters and sewing clothes without patterns, guides or instructions, making yogurt, baking bread, churning butter, making charcoal, weaving bee hives from bamboo canes and taking care of bee swarms. Some of these became second nature to us and we continue them today. Our yogurt culture dates from the day when our family arrived in this country in

Here we stand in what's left of the Apostolic Church, site of our Darindos celebrations. Its roof had never been finished so services were held in summer when it rarely rained. From left are Alberta, cousin, Aurora, Louisa and Alex.

Photo: Richard Furno

1951. That year, Louisa was nine, but even she has learned many of these skills as we perpetuated them in this country. She calls these chores "maintenance".

Although Anna and I had chores, at our young age our responsibilities were limited. We were too young to prune trees or bake bread. I had to water Mom's two dozen potted plants every other day, fetch pitchers of fresh water from Frank's spring, count the goats as they returned from the mountain, secure the barn and keep an eye on Anna. I tried to ignore this last when I could get away with it. Anna loved cleaning the barn, a task no one asked her to do. I suspect she enjoyed sweeping the marble-size goat droppings with a heather broom that was kept in the corner of the barn. We both hated guarding Mom's bowl of custard chilling in the brook next to the house. In our minds, the 20 minutes was 20 hours but then, custard was one of our favorite desserts so we endured the ordeal.

Many of us also learned survival skills. Most young people could survive on the mountain for days, a necessity if they were hunting, became stranded or lost. People knew which berries and herbs were nonpoisonous and edible. They knew how to start a fire with dry leaves and two pieces of flint. Since most young men carried small pocket knives, they could easily make a trap and capture small animals. Later, in New Jersey, Anna and I learned that skill from Pop.

Seasonal Life

In Bitias, seasons determined the pattern of life. Our winters were quiet and mild, yet, it snowed several times a year, the kind where all traces disappeared from the rooftops and dirt roads by noon. We did not have central heating, but our windows had southern exposure and rooms warmed up quickly on clear days. We also had a charcoal pit in the living room surrounded with comfortable mats and soft cushions, our favorite spot during winter nights. With no TV or radio, we sat around the pit listening to wonderful tales about giants and eagles transporting people to exotic places.

Our favorite story teller was a young man in his twenties named Taminos, the Pied Piper of our village. We would prepare our favorite refreshments of popcorn, pomegranate, figs and nuts, and then follow him from house to house ready for long winter evenings as he weaved his magical yarns.

Christmas Eve, January 5, was a special event. The elders of both churches, with some other male members, visited every house in the village singing the same Christmas carol with all 12 verses. We sat around our charcoal pit and waited for the carolers. Once they arrived and lined up near the door, Pop joined the group and sang with them. One by one they wished us "Merry Christmas" and proceeded to the next house. Almost every household had some monetary gift for them. These contributions were quietly distributed to the needy families in the village.

Christmas was a day of worship. The church "bells", made of iron bars, would ring in the morning calling the parishioners to church service. Then families visited each other and shared Christmas dinner together. We did not exchange gifts or decorate trees, instead, we just made sure our homes were spotless for the holy day.

New Year was a different story. It was the equivalent of today's Halloween. Preparations were made long before, but for the children the fun started on New Year's Eve. We put on our homemade costumes and masks and trudged through the muddy, dark streets visiting only those houses where we expected special treats. For us, the special treats were oranges, but we usually ended up with some nuts and wormy dry figs. We giggled with our friends while adults humored us by pretending they couldn't guess our true identities. We had fun getting dirty and knowing that no scolding was waiting for us. Mom simply had a kettle of hot water ready to give us our New Year bath.

Spring came early in Bitias. By mid-February, wild flowers bloomed and changed the fields to a palette of pink, orange, purple, yellow and white. In spite of their lilliputian size, the most fragrant of these were violets. The spring wildflowers signaled the time for our annual school picnic. Held at the mountain top, we hiked to Tataralang and Damlajog, two historic sites where our elders had taken refuge from the Ottoman army in 1915.

For the picnic, families gathered at the school and proceeded up the mountain carrying empty baskets to collect flowers. Our lunch consisted of *tonir* bread, hard boiled eggs and dried figs wrapped in a square piece of cloth that was folded into a loop to carry on one's arm or tie around one's waist for the long trip up the mountain, a challenging climb I always looked forward to. Water, was provided by springs and some ancient wells located along our path. We always ate our lunch at Damlajog spring which offered a lovely view of the Mediterranean Sea. Most adults preferred to rest there while we would roll down the hill, wander around gathering violets and do anything else that we fancied. There were always some knowledgeable students who knew where the best violets grew. They also instructed us about different trees, their names and their uses. We would arrive back home with baskets of wilted violets, pebbles and bits of bark.

In February, we also celebrated "Darindos", the Saturday before Lent. I have since read that, in fact, the Darindos celebration in Musa Dagh dates back to our pagan days. We gathered huge piles of wood and brush and carried them to the grounds of the Armenian Apostolic Church, the highest point in the village. Pop always made sure that we had an ample pile of brush. He tied the brush tightly with a cord forming a neat bundle to make it easy for us to drag through the streets and up the endless steps to the church grounds. After the church service, the congregation gathered around the wood pile and the newlywed men kindled the wood with their candles. Everyone clapped and began to sing patriotic songs.

Once the fire lost some of its force, the young men showed off their prowess by jumping over the flames while the multitude cheered and teased them on. At the end of the merrymaking, we returned to our homes with lighted candles and half-burnt sticks. That night, we lighted our lamps with the candles and threw the sticks into our orchards. Sometimes we buried a stick under a favorite tree. Using a stick as a talisman, we hoped good luck would bless our orchards and double the fruit harvest. Once a young cousin brought his half-burnt stick home and instead of whisking it into the orchard, he threw it over the house hoping for additional blessing for his family. His innocent action almost burned down his house.

Easter was referred to as the "big holiday" in contrast to Christmas which was the "small holiday." Days before Easter, Mom gathered the outer skins of onions to use as dye. These, she boiled with eggs, coloring them to various shades of deep orange to light brown. On Saturday, the children started an Easter egg contest at every corner of the village. Each child had a couple of hard-boiled, russet eggs with which to challenge friends to an egg-cracking competition. The object was to hold the egg firmly and expose just a tiny spot on the narrow end. The challenger eyed the spot and tried to crack the shell gently with his own egg. If he cracked your egg, you turned your egg around hoping the egg's other end would make you that round's winner. The person holding the last uncracked egg was the winner and collected all the cracked eggs to take home. Losers looked forward to victory the following year.

Today's after-church celebrations might include Easter egg hunts as well as Easter baskets filled with plastic eggs, toys and candy, and even gifts of sophisticated video games. I contrast the games I see my nephew play on his computer with our simple egg-cracking game which we have had him enthusiastically compete in for almost 25 years.

After our Easter church services, families gathered for a big Sunday dinner, often consisting of stuffed shoulder of lamb, cheese bread, holiday rings and baklava rolls (*ahyagai, banderoom hootz, peegegh, and boormo*). To this day, we continue to prepare these holiday dishes, and play the traditional game of egg-cracking with eggs we've dyed with onion skins.

Home Life

Mom woke up every morning to do battle with her list of chores: get the children ready for school, clean the house, sparkle the glass in the lanterns and fill them with kerosene, fetch jugs of water from Frank's spring, sweep the barn, the yard and the front street, fill the cistern with water for the thirsty goats before they return from the mountain, knead and bake the *tonir* bread before the children return from school for lunch. These were her morning responsibilities and were probably pretty typical of every household.

During her morning chores, she might be interrupted by visitors. Some were relatives who visited frequently, even daily. Uncle Mo would stop by soon after we left for school to check on his sister and sometimes stay long enough for a cup of Turkish coffee. Aunt Myroom, also Mom's sister, usually visited in the afternoon and sometimes we found her dozing in a corner in the living room when we came home from school.

Maran Moorkayr was a widow who had lost her husband in World War I and was raising her only son alone. She came and went as she chose and, without being asked, did everything for Mom that needed to be done. She bathed us, scolded us, fed us and teased us. She was like a grandmother to us.

Villagers sometimes stopped to share news or just chat and gossip. Mom welcomed everyone and knew all the gossip. Besides these daily messengers, Maran Moorkayr was the source of the stories of all major events in Bitias. Every morning on her way to our house, she made several strategic stops before arriving at our door.

Because we were one of the families whose larder was always full, we helped those less fortunate when they came to our door. Some visitors asked for a favor or for much-needed items that we readily fulfilled; "Auntie," (every married woman in Bitias was everyone's auntie) "could we borrow a cup of sugar?", "a loaf of bread?", "how about a bowl of pickles?", "do you have any leftover fruit from Chaghlaghan?" "our fire is out, can you spare some coals?"

Book Club and Ponies

Late afternoons, especially during the winter months, life in the village slowed down. Mom's 'book club' met during those quiet afternoons. Since we did not have a public library and since most people did not have books with the exception of the Bible, Mom's club was limited to a single copy of the selected book. The books often came from Pop's small collection.

The women passed the single copy around the circle and each person read a paragraph aloud, followed by a discussion. Because of the Great War, Mom's education stopped with the second grade so she hadn't learned to read well, but somehow she was still able to take part. After returning home from school, Anna and I would sit in a corner and listen attentively. We spent one winter listening to Victor Hugo's *Les Miserables*. With the rarity of books, such stories became precious. For us, as the women talked about poor Cosette, Jean Valjean and Javert, the characters took on real personalities.

As the sun would begin to set behind Musa Dagh, life picked up again. People returned from the fields, and groups of women headed to the spring carrying their empty jugs on their shoulders. The spring provided drinking water and served as a village gossip center as well. Shepherds blocked the streets with hundreds of bleating goats and barking dogs. The entire scene looked like bedlam to the inexperienced eye. To us, it was a wonder as we watched each group of animals separate from the herd and follow the path to their own barn without any coaxing from the shepherd or the herding dogs.

Our goats dashed to the stone cisterns, drank their fill, then headed to the barn. Once inside, they were counted, milked and fed. The next morning, they dashed out of the barn to join the herd, urinating and fertilizing the village streets on their way to pastures high on the mountain.

Pop was usually the last person to return to the village carrying basketfuls of fruits and vegetables from Chaghlaghan on his back as well as some kind of treat for us. Our favorite gift was the occasional small stone he would find that had a hole in its center. We had a collection of these and called them 'ponies.' We tied a string through the holes and dragged them behind us.

These 'ponies' fared better than the live one Pop bought for Anna when she was six or seven years old. When she was two, every evening, as soon as Pop got home, she would start wailing for a ride on the neighbor's pony. This became a riding ritual, and only Pop could be her escort. The entire neighborhood watched this spectacle as it went on year after year. In time, she developed a yearning for her own pony. She would periodically raise an accusatory glance at Pop and announce, "Dad, you never bought me a pony." This might take place when we had company.

Finally, he did it! He brought home a pony to take Anna for daily rides. Meantime, he would also take it to Chaghlaghan every day while Anna was at school. This pleased Mom. She hoped heavy baskets of vegetables would be loaded on the pony's back. But Pop couldn't bear the idea of burdening the pony. Not once did he share the load with the pony. He continued to carry everything on his back while the pony romped gleefully in front of him.

The day came when Anna wanted to ride her pony by herself! Pop lifted her and carefully settled her on the pony's back. Anna grinned, all happy and brave. But after taking a few steps, the pony kicked its hind legs, threw Anna on the ground and took off. Frightened, we rushed to her but Anna did not cry. She just felt betrayed. The pony never returned and Anna never mentioned live ponies again.

Silk Industry

With the sprouting of the first tender leaves on the mulberry trees, the silk industry preoccupied the village from mid-March to mid-May. It was one of the major cash industries in Bitias.

Long before the first larvae hatched, people emptied a room, whitewashed it from top to bottom and lined bamboo mats on scaffolding extending up to the ceiling. The silk worms lived and produced their precious cocoons on these mats. Each day the room had to be cleaned and the worms fed their diet of mulberry leaves, morning, noon and evening. They were also protected from changes in temperature, an often difficult task. But the end result of the intensive care would be rewarded by a high price brought by the collected, mature cocoons.

Gathering the cocoons and scraping their loose threads was usually a community affair. Neighbors and relatives worked together before the silk moth tore a hole and emerged thereby making the silk thread worthless. People wanted to complete this task by dusk and transfer the responsibility of caring for the cocoons to the merchants who traveled from household to household weighing, loading and transporting the cargo to the markets in Antioch. Once the owner was paid for the cocoons, people were relieved from this intensive chore and ready for a celebration. The households who pocketed the profits supplied trays of halva and *tonir* bread for the villagers. More halva was consumed in Bitias during those few days than for the rest of the year.

When I was about eleven years old, Anna and I decided to start our own silk worm business. Failing to gain our parents support, we convinced an aunt to part with one of her tiny mulberry leaves covered with a few "seeds" (larvae). I cradled the leaf in my palms and presented it to Mom.

"What is that?" She began. "Do you realize there are more than 100 larvae on that leaf? Where are you going to put them and who is going to take care of them? Don't you realize you're destroying those precious worms? Return that to your aunt, now!"

Anna started crying and I tried to look as pathetic as possible holding the little leaf in my palm. We didn't budge. Finally, "Okay," she said, "you can keep it tonight, but tomorrow it goes." She walked away probably thinking that by tomorrow we would realize the huge responsibility and give up without any further coaxing. The minute she left, we knew we had won! Of course we had no intention of returning our worms.

Anna stopped crying and returned to playing with her friends. We were certain that Pop would be our ally. And sure enough, he set up a little table covered it with a clean towel in the corner of a room and told us to deposit the precious cargo. With a mulberry tree in the front yard, we felt confident about feeding the worms. With Pop in our corner, we couldn't fail.

Within a couple of weeks, a large platform replaced the little table and an empty room served as the worm habitat. Mom soon participated in our venture by supplying us with a clean sheet to cover the rough wooden board and helping us with the daily care of our silk worms.

We pampered them! We carefully cleaned the room each day. Instead of feeding them three times, we insisted on feeding them fresh leaves five times a day. Our silk worms got big and fat! Soon, even Mom began to brag about them. They became the talk of the village. Merchants approached our parents and suggested that the cocoons should be sold for their eggs instead of their silk but for the following year's crop.

Anna and I were thrilled with our enterprise. Then, in the midst of our anticipation, I came down with the measles and missed the final stages of our business venture. Covered with hundreds of red spots, an ear ache, and a raging fever, I was isolated within a cocoon of my own while the world spun around me.

When family and friends were able to visit, I was happy to have company. One uncle, a merchant by trade, was my most frequent visitor and each time he came, he leaned over my red face and whispered about the gold coins that the cocoon would bring. In my feverish state, I dreamt about pots of gold waiting for my sister and me.

Ultimately, my uncle did sell the cocoons in Antioch. He had promised to give us the money the following day. The tomorrows kept adding up and finally, a week after his Antioch trip, Mom gave each of us a large silver coin equivalent to half a dollar. But Anna and I knew that the money came from Mom rather than our uncle.

Chicks and Goats

We did not stay crushed for long. It was about this time that one of our hens had disappeared for several weeks and we thought it had been snatched by a fox Then, it appeared in the yard trailed by a dozen chicks. We were jubilant! We began to name and claim the various chicks as our very own. We followed the mother hen from a distance and fed our favorite chicks with tender *tonir* bread. This went on for a couple of weeks when another event grabbed our attention.

Newborn baby goats or kids held special significance in every family. They were like having noted guests. Of course, they were even better since they never left. Fifty percent of them were born in the barn and the other half on the mountain where the herds would be grazing. They arrived back at the village riding on the shoulders of shepherds or nestled inside their *abbas* with their heads peeking out and bleating all the way down the mountain. The *abba* was a woven goat-hair coat that shepherds wore loosely over their shirts. Shepherds secured their belts over this loose fitting garment creating pockets inside above the belt. There, they would stuff their lunch, necessities and, on these occasions, baby goats to keep them warm, dry or carry them long distances. When we saw the shepherd entering the village, sometimes loaded with three kids, we forgot everything and ran to carry a bleating kid to its home.

School and Summer Vacation

When our primers were in tatters and clumsily glued together, our slates cracked and our notebooks left with no empty pages, we knew that summer vacation was nearly upon us. We didn't have final exams, report cards, or parent conferences. The first time I received a report card was when I started attending the American High School in Aleppo, Syria. The closest thing to a parent conference in Bitias was usually initiated by a grandmother when she appeared before the teacher dragging a grandson by the collar and demanding that he get a beating for some transgression committed at home. I never

Alberta (left) and Anna have a firm hold on their pet goat, in photo taken around 1933. Every year, they each claimed a goat for themselves.

witnessed a student being beaten in our school, but once in a while a teacher would use a ruler on a student's shoulder. The following year we would return with new textbooks and with the old classmates to continue with minor changes in our curriculum.

School ended with a "hantess", a play or performance. Students put on their Sunday best and recited poems, sang songs, duets and solos. Naturally, some students froze on stage and forgot their verses. That was never Anna's problem or mine. Once, Anna tip toed up to the stage, spread her arms and, imitating our minister, began to bless the 'congregation'.

Once the school closed its doors for the summer, we impatiently waited for the arrival of our summer residents from the cities. The three hotels in Bitias provided accommodations for visitors who wanted to spend a short time visiting the village. Anna and I waited for the arrival of one particular family that rented rooms in our house. The mother with her three children arrived and stayed for the entire summer. The father, a doctor, visited a couple of weekends but aunts and cousins seemed to come and go all the time. Once the family arrived, we children eyed each other for a few moments and then began to catch up by asking questions and relating tales. Any schedules for French or embroidery lessons that their mother might have planned for her daughters were scuttled within a week. Our summer friends joined us for old and new games and for exploring the woods and splashing in cool springs. Women often spent mornings in bazaars bargaining with Turkmen merchants from neighboring villages.

Our main street had several kerosene lamps perched on wooden poles at several intersections making it possible for the outdoor coffee houses to stay open until about midnight. The most popular was Hatum Agha's Coffee House next to Frank's spring. It featured a pool, excellent location and, most importantly, cold beer, soda, olives, mezza or hors d'oeuvres and fresh baked *tonir* bread. One could also have a cup of Turkish coffee with friends and expect the proprietor to tell one's fortune at the end. Once the coffee was finished, the person tipped the cup upside down on the saucer to allow the grounds to run out. The fortune teller used the intricate patterns inside the cup to spin some fabulous or improbable tales or perhaps an inevitable type of prediction.

With the influx of so many summer visitors came trash! Our garbage collector, one man and his donkey, increased his services to several times a week during this, his peak season. He went from house to house, emptied full cans of garbage into baskets hoisted on the donkey and carried them to the dump. The "baledieh", the village committee, swept the main street, but each family was responsible for the area around their houses. This latter responsibility fell to the children who often coaxed their summer friends to join in.

Our streets didn't have names and our houses weren't numbered since villagers knew everybody by name. Sections of the village had names and they were frequently used as reference. Without regular mail service our mail arrived in Antioch where it was picked up by muleteers who went to the city several times a week to carry cargo from the village and pick up orders for the individual families. They usually returned by dusk on the same day and members of the families distributed the orders and the mail throughout the village.

Our life was not only seasonal, but fairly predictable. Once in a while the "dellool", the town crier, disturbed our routine. He went from section to section shouting his announcement. His version of "hear ye, hear ye" sounded more like "whether you hear me or not, you are responsible for my message." His message usually declared either the arrival of the tax collector or of some dignitary.

The Experiences and Stories from World War I

Anna and I were born and lived well after the infamous events of World War I. We were not the victims of the atrocities of that time, nevertheless, war stories were built into the fabric of the village and were never far from any adult's lips. Tragic images were deeply imbedded in the minds of the survivors and when they surfaced we overheard the circumstances and tribulations that surrounded friends and relatives that perished. Even for those Armenians who didn't live in Turkey during World War I, the experience of parents, grandparents and relative left their impact. My sister Louisa, for example, was born in Syria in 1942, but she still heard enough to ask the difficult questions that were so heart-rending to answer.

For Armenians, and for many others, "Musa Dagh" is synonymous for the Armenian struggle for survival during World War I. It was at Musa Dagh where Armenians fought off the Turkish Army over a period of a month and a half. In 1934, it was fictionalized by Franz Werfel in his novel, *The Forty Days of Musa Dagh*. But, for us, it was home, not just a place that existed during a World War I confrontation.

As we grew up, inevitably, we found ourselves listening raptly to the stories of friends and family members who managed to hold off the Ottoman army long enough to be rescued by passing French warships. Of course, if the Ottoman army contingency had been larger the Armenians would have been overrun. Indeed, just when rescue came, a larger Ottoman force was on its way to put down the resistance. The Armenians on Musa Dagh had fought well enough, desperately enough, and long enough to ultimately survive.

Other accounts told of marches through the Syrian desert during which many perished. Our Mother was one of those who survived that march. Throughout her life, she seldom wanted to talk about the march and the starvation in Hama that caused the deaths of most of her family.

Mom, who made that march at age nine, could scarcely maintain her composure when relating the events of that time. Rather than talking of the tragedies again and again, she preferred to leave it behind. But almost as if it seeps up from the ground, the experiences emerged from our parents and relatives who fought so hard to survive.

In 1915, Pop had six living brothers, both parents and his grandmother, Sima. He had gone to America years before the war on the advice of his father. His oldest brother, with his wife and their two daughters, and Pop's youngest brother, followed him to America.

The rest remained in Bitias. When the deportation occurred, all but Sima made and survived the march to Hama; she was killed while climbing the mountain. In Hama, two brothers were recruited by the Ottomans and were never seen again. Except for one brother and his nine-year-old son, the others died of disease or starvation.

Of course, we carry not just the memory of Musa Dagh, but also of the Armenian genocide. Unfortunately, the Turks deny it to this day and consequently, it becomes more difficult to leave behind – the forgotten genocide.

Yet, there is an important caveat to this story. The orders to the Ottoman armies to commit the deportations and genocide came from the three leaders of the Empire; Enver, Talaat and Jemal. During our family's crises, many Turkish friends reached out to help as much as they could. Many Turks throughout the country did the same. To blame the Turkish people for the terrible events of 1915 is a mistake.

Chaghlaghan Reborn

Pop's love and devotion for Chaghlaghan didn't end when we left Turkey in 1939. Almost twenty years later, he began building walls and planting gardens on the half acre of our New Jersey home. We watched as he transformed our rocky hillside into a miniature Chaghlaghan orchard with its peaches, apricots, cherries, grapes and vegetables. He used strings and sticks, to create the perfect arcs for his level, stone walls, some of which stood five feet tall. He himself did not stand much taller! He left just enough room on the land to build our house.

When we sold our New Jersey home, two surveyors spent ten days measuring and tracing his walls. They marveled not only at the architecture and design, but the fact that the walls were built without mortar. During the 25 years we lived there, the walls never budged from frost. Pop was 70 years old when he began this project.

The Recipes of Musa Dagh

Our only group photo dates from 1978 at Richard's and Louisa's wedding. From left, Alberta, Richard, Pop (Samuel), Louisa, Mom (Victoria) and Anna.

Chaghlaghan Reborn — Again

Our one and only nephew and our parent's only grandchild, was born in 1981. Pop was 93, Mom was 75. Our family picked up and moved to join Louisa, her husband Richard and newborn Alex in Maryland. We bought a house with a rocky, sloping yard where we could terrace a third Chaghlaghan. Our quarter acre has no fruit trees. But the garden overflows with the usual culprits — flowers, tomatoes, parsley, eggplant, peppers, Swiss chard, string beans, sweet peas, *gooloogoos*, beets, cucumbers, herbs and the occasional odd vegetable. We even listen to the gurgling water of a nearby creek in the common area next to us while we tend the garden. With canning, freezing and sprouting seeds in the garage, gardening stretches throughout the year.

And finally...

Each meal we prepare dates back to Bitias and the region of clustered villages on Musa Dagh. Louisa teases us about cooking without recipes, how the dishes reside only in Anna's head and how I've only been able to pick up a few. Alex has gained interest and occasionally comes over on weekend mornings and learns how to cook some particular item. For him, Anna has patience. Now, he can cook *baghash* (page 30). Even Louisa can't do that!

A few years ago, Louisa and I decided we needed a Musa Dagh cookbook. All we had to do was recruit Anna! That took some real convincing, but when she said OK, she pitched right in, cooking up whatever we needed to record. So here's our cookbook! It seems to us a good final product from Mom's original kitchen.

My deepest and sincerest thanks to Louisa and to her husband Richard for converting my stream-of-consciousness writings into intelligible text.

Today, left to right: Louisa, Anna and Alberta

Glossary

Bitias – Our village, one of the six main villages of Musa Dagh, about 10 miles west of Antioch.

Bulgur – Wheat kernel which has been boiled, dried and ground into several sizes from 1, the smallest to 4, the largest or most coarse.

Chaghlaghan– The Magzanian family orchard several miles north of Bitias village where a large spring powered two flour mills before World War I. Its name has migrated into Turkish for the cafe at the site, called "Caglayan".

Constantinople – Changed to Istanbul in 1453 by Sultan Mehmed II. Change became official in 1930. Fourth century capital city of Emperor Constantine.

Darindos – Pagan holiday celebrated in Bitias with bonfires and music. Celebrated on Saturday before the first day of Lent.

Havoush – Courtyard.

Jebel Akrah – Mountain in northwest Syria near Kessab.

Jebel Musa – Arabic for Musa Dagh.

Kara Chai – Turkish. Tributary of the Orontes River where the boundary of Musa Dagh (Suedia) starts.

Kima – The Kistinik word for "filling", either meat or meatless, in Musa Dagh dishes.

Kistinik – Native Armenian dialect of Musa Dagh. The literal meaning of "Kistinik" is "Christian."

Mezza – Hors d'oeuvre, appetizer.

Musa Dagh – Turkish for Mountain of Moses.

Musa Daghtsi – a native of Musa Dagh.

Musa Ler – Standard Armenian for "Musa Dagh". In Armenian, "ler" means "mountain".

Sanjak – A political subdivision of the Ottoman Empire. The Musa Dagh area fell into the Alexandretta Sanjak. After World War I, the League of Nations split off the area of Syria from the Empire granting it to the French as a mandate. It included the Alexandretta Sanjak. A plebiscite was held in 1939 after which the area was transferred to Turkey. It is now the province of Hatay. Syria still does not accept the validity of the transfer.

Tataralang – Area on Musa Dagh mountain. Literally, "the land of Tartars."

Tonir Bread – Musa Dagh bread baked in a brick pit oven (tiner).

Index

A

B

Beans and Legumes
   chick peas (see Chick peas)
   fava bean pilaf, 83
   fava bean salad with yogurt, 41
   fava beans and onions, 74
   green bean, bulgur pilaf, 84
   green bean, meat stew, 69
   green bean, bulgur potato pilaf, 85
   green bean, potato, zucchini stew, 64
   kidney bean (red), salads, 42
   lentil pilaf, 86
   lentil, yogurt pilaf soup, 63
   lentil soup with barley, 50
   lentil (red split) soup, 49
   mixed and walnuts, 73
   multi-bean, potato soup, 52
   multi-bean, Swiss chard soup, 53
   multi-legume stew, 66

Bulgur
   bean-potato pilaf, 85
   fava bean pilaf, 83
   green bean pilaf, 84
   lamb mixture (*keufteh*), 111
   lentil pilaf, 86
   meat dumplings (*kaloors*), 58
   meatless filling, 89
   mixed vegetable pilaf, 85
   molasses or honey dessert, 133
   multi-bean, Swiss chard soup, 53
   multi-legume stew, 66
   pilaf with chick peas, 81
   pilaf with meat, 82
   potato, 71
   potato pilaf, 83
   salad with cooked vegetables, 43
   stuffed meat patties, 114
   tabouli, 42

C

Cabbage
   eggplant zucchini pilaf (mixed vegetable pilaf), 85
   leaves, stuffed, 91
   meat filling for, 88
   meatless filling for, 89
   mixed vegetable pilaf, 85
   pink pickles, 121
   soup, 48

Chick peas
   bulgur pilaf, 81
   eggplant, 69
   galagacia soup, 51
   head and tongue soup, 55
   hummus, 38
   mixed beans with walnuts, 73
   multi-bean, Swiss chard soup, 53
   multi-legume stew, 66
   rice filling, 89
   roasted, 126, 127
   potato multi-bean soup, 52
   tomato soup with dumplings, 62
   tongue, see also "head and tongue soup"
   tongue and tripe soup, 56
   walnuts, see "mixed beans with walnuts"
   wheat berries, 133
   yogurt, zucchini and meat stew, 65

Cucumber
   pickles, 122
   soup with yogurt, 64

D

Dumplings
   baked, 96
   for yogurt soup, *agantch*, 58
   for soups, *kaloor*, 60
   fried and syrup, 136

tomato soup, 62
yogurt soup, 61

E

Eggplant
baba ganoush, 38
chick peas, 67
baked, with meat, 95
baked, with tomato and garlic, 77
fillings for, 88
fried, 77
fried with eggs, 78
grilled, 75
kebab, 100
meat, 68
mixed vegetable pilaf, 85
roasted, 76
salad, 45
stuffed, 91, 105
yogurt salad, 44

F-J

K

Kafta (Kofta) - see Keufteh, 109

L

M

Meat dishes, 95; mostly use lamb but beef can be substituted.

N

Nuts
pistachios, 141
walnuts, 45, 60, 73, 89, 111, 130, 131, 133-135, 139, 141

O

Onion dishes
sautéed with potatoes, 71
spinach, 73

P

Parsley dishes
egg patties, 76
tabouli, 42

Potato dishes (also see Potatoes, 71)
bean, bulgur pilaf, 85
bulgur pilaf, 83
green bean, zucchini stew, 64
salad, 41
multi-bean soup, 52

Q

R

Rice
lentil soup, 49
meat, meatless fillings, 88, 89
pilaf, 81
pudding, 129
stuffed grape leaves, cabbage, other vegetables, 90-94
stuffed shoulder of lamb, 108
tomato soup, 54
tripe, 106

S

Spinach
with onions, 73
Soup de Paris, 48

Swiss chard
multi-bean soup, 53
stuffed (like grape leaves), 89, 94

T

Tabouli, 42

Tomato
    baked with vegetables and meat, 96
    grilled, 75
    meat filling, 88
    pickles, 122
    relish or sauce, 123
    rice meatless filling, 89
    soup, 54
    soup with dumplings, 62
    stuffed, 93

U-V

W

Wheat, shelled
    cabbage soup, 48
    cooked skinless, 48 (recipe), 48, 50, 54, 63, 72, 73, 104
    lamb, 104
    lentil soup, 50
    mixed beans with walnuts, 73
    potato, 72
    preparation, 48
    vegetable soup, 54
    yogurt soup, 63

X

Y

Yogurt, 21
    Ann's cottage cheese, 25
    cabbage soup, 48
    cucumber soup, 64
    drained (yogurt cheese), 23
    drink, 19
    dumplings for soup, 58
    dumplings, baked, 96
    eggplant, 44
    eggplant (roasted), 76
    fava beans, 41
    galagacia soup, 50
    garlic sauce, 123
    lentil pilaf soup, 63
    making, 22
    milk desert, 134
    onions, 73, 120
    soup, 58
    soup with bulgur-meat dumplings, 61
    soup with skinless whole wheat, 63
    spinach, 73
    zucchini and meat stew, 65

Z

Zucchini
    baked vegetables with meat, 96
    cabbage soup, 48
    fried, 78
    green bean, potato stew, 64
    grilled, 75
    meat and yogurt stew, 65
    mixed vegetable pilaf, 85
    pilaf, 81, 85
    potato, green bean stew, 64
    stuffed, 91